W9-AFE-617

MASTER DRAWINGS FROM CALIFORNIA COLLECTIONS   Edited by Juergen Schulz

University Art Museum, University of California, Berkeley   Distributed by New York Graphic Society Ltd., Greenwich, Connecticut

Exhibition dates: 30 April to 2 June 1968 in honor of University of California Centennial, 1868-1968

CONTENTS

This publication commemorates the Centennial of the University of California and, in addition, celebrates an important stage of maturity in the development of the University Art Museum. Despite temporary exhibition and administrative facilities, pending completion of the splendid new building now in construction, the Museum has gone ahead with this major project. Its completion and success were made possible by the cooperation of the students and faculty of the Art History Department of the University. This kind of joint venture is certainly the rationale for a university museum, and we are especially proud that this precedent has been set so early in the Museum's history.

"Master Drawings from California Collections" thus results from the combination of two factors: first, the expertise of a scholar directing his students in the research phases of the project, and second, the expertise of the Museum staff in planning and arranging loans, careful handling and display, and experience in publishing procedures. A collaboration of this nature is possible only in the largest museums or in museums connected with a teaching system.

Our interest in California drawing collections is essentially twofold. The study and collection of master drawings has traditionally represented a very sophisticated level of connoisseurship. Thus the focus on drawings in the State indicates in an important way the educational pre-eminence of its hundred-year-old University. Furthermore, many of the works in California collections have not been published previously, and some of them have never been publicly exhibited. This situation provided a rare opportunity for students to work with important material, to develop opinions in the process of facing new art historical problems, and perhaps most important, to have their opinions published in a widely-read source. This exhibition constitutes the first survey of master drawings from California collections, and should become an important reference work for scholars.

The drawings include only works executed before the modern period, because the earlier drawings seem to form a body of works related both in conception and feeling. The drawings range from two early sixteenth-century sheets by Carpaccio and the Master of the Mühldorf Altar, to drawings by Géricault and Delacroix from the first half of the nineteenth century. The drawings were carefully selected from a large group available in California, and represent a culling of drawings most suited in quality and interest to an exhibition of this kind. In the process of developing this exhibition it was particularly impressive to find such a large number of drawings in private and public collections. Although the largest number of drawings are Italian, the general distribution among various countries and historical periods fairly represents the available resources.

We have noted that the exhibition is very much a group effort. Juergen Schulz, Professor of the History of Art and the Museum's Curator of Renaissance Art, provided his knowledge and understanding throughout the project. He worked enthusiastically with his students and with the

Museum staff through all phases of preparing the catalogue, which he edited with so much scholarship. We are also grateful to the students in Professor Schulz's seminar for writing catalogue entries based on their study of the drawings: Donald Ackland, Elizabeth De Gall, Sungmii Han, Susan King, Carolyn Malone, Lynn Ostling, Mae Quan, Natalie Rosenberg, Marcus Sopher, June Steingart, Elizabeth Sullivan, Michael Tepper, Keith Thoreen, Diana Turner and Wallace Weston.

Svetlana Alpers, Assistant Professor of the History of Art and Curator of Baroque Art for the Museum, helped Professor Schulz and the Museum staff in selecting the drawings for the exhibition. The entire project has been supervised for the Museum by Susan Rannells, Exhibition Assistant, whose devotion to the details of the exhibition and publication have made it possible. Brenda Richardson, Exhibition Assistant, provided editorial skills in preparing the catalogue for publication. Lawrence Dinnean, Museum Preparator, skillfully supervised the handling of these delicate materials. The publication itself has been subsidized by the Office of Centennial Celebration.

Many people helped at various stages of the project, and we are particularly grateful to Florence Dauber, Alfred Moir, Agnes Mongan, Alfred Neumeyer and Jacob Zeitlin. We also thank the various collectors who graciously permitted us to view their drawings in preparation for this project, although their collections may not be represented in the exhibition. The lenders have been especially generous, not only in their loans, but also in aiding students to obtain information about the drawings. Museums and individuals are justifiably reluctant to lend drawings because of their physically delicate nature, so we are most indebted to the good will of all the lenders for providing these generous loans.

Tom L. Freudenheim *Assistant Director, University Art Museum*

INTRODUCTION

The collecting of drawings as works of art rather than as curiosities began in the Italian Renaissance. The Medici owned drawings, according to the inventories of their collections taken in the 1490's. The Venetian lover of antiquities and modern works of art, Cardinal Domenico Grimani, left drawings to his heirs, as one can infer from an inventory of the possessions of one of them, Cardinal Marino Grimani, taken in 1528. However, these early connoisseurs did not collect sketches systematically with the purpose of forming a collection broadly representative of a particular epoch or school of artists.

The first collector who consciously pursued such a goal was the father of modern art history, Giorgio Vasari (1511-1574), the author of the *Lives of the Artists*. Vasari began collecting material for these *Lives* — lists of works of art and biographical notes — quite early in his career,

8

long before he had actually conceived the project of the book. In a similar spirit of cultivating the great, immediate past of Florentine art, he collected drawings by masters of the fourteenth, fifteenth and sixteenth centuries. In time the collection came to include one or more sheets by almost every artist he had found worthy of mention in the *Lives,* and in the enlarged second edition of the book (1568) he frequently refers to the collection of drawings. It was kept in five large folio volumes, in which the drawings were stuck down, one or more to the page, and framed in ornate architectural surrounds in pen and wash.

Vasari's pattern was soon imitated. Later sixteenth-century amateurs throughout Europe began to collect drawings, and usually in a similar fashion as Vasari. This is not the place to follow out in detail the history of drawing collecting. Suffice it to say that the seventeenth and eighteenth centuries were its heyday. Methods of mounting drawings changed — in France, for instance, the technique of sticking drawings on loose mounts, with a repeated border for a frame, was invented and from there introduced to other centers of collecting, like England. Collections numbering several thousand sheets were formed, and changed hands repeatedly by private sale, public auction, and courteous exchanges between fellow amateurs.

The collecting taste was still widespread in the nineteenth century, but as the value of drawings appreciated and as styles changed and the art of the past became institutionalized, private individuals found it progressively more difficult to assemble large collections of old master drawings. The individual collector was replaced by institutions — museums and libraries, the older ones of which had acquired large drawing collections at the moment of their foundation as parts of royal or other estates that had formed their nucleus. The Louvre acquired what had been the French royal collection, the Uffizi what had been the Tuscan grand ducal collection, the Hermitage what had been the collection of the Czars. Other museums, without such an inheritance, followed suit by building drawing collections with purchases made on the art market.

In this way the major drawing cabinets of Europe and the eastern United States came into being in the nineteenth and early twentieth centuries, and have continued to grow ever since. In the case of drawings, as generally in the fine arts, the bulk of the treasures that have come to America are concentrated in the East. The great drawing collections of the United States are in The Metropolitan Museum of Art and The Pierpont Morgan Library at New York, and the Fogg Art Museum at Cambridge. But California has shared in this development, starting later and growing more slowly than the Atlantic region, but making a not negligible contribution to American collecting nevertheless.

Drawings have been collected in California since the 1870's, and at an increasing pace since the emergence of numerous museums in the urban centers of the state in the middle of this century. The earliest, and still one of the finest drawing collections in California, is that of the E. B. Crocker Art Gallery in Sacramento. It was formed as the result of a whirlwind campaign by Edwin Crocker (1818-1875) to build a significant collection of drawings and paintings for his adoptive city of Sacramento.

Crocker was born in upper New York State, and worked first as a civil engineer in the construction of railways in New York (a brother became one of the founders of the Central Pacific Railway). In the 1840's he turned to law, and in 1852 arrived in Sacramento to begin a successful career as an attorney and as a figure in California state politics. He served as a justice on the State Supreme Court in 1863-1864, and acted as chief counsel for the Central Pacific Railway from 1864 to 1869.

It was only at the end of his career that he began to purchase systematically and in quantity both drawings and paintings with the intention of leaving them as a collection to the City of Sacramento. He traveled to Europe with his family, and established himself at Dresden. From there he bought both personally and through agents at Dresden, Munich and Düsseldorf. In a very short time he had assembled a collection of, among other objects, almost one thousand drawings. The majority were drawings of the Italian, German and Netherlandish schools (respectively, 350, 250, and 200 sheets). A number of them, including numbers *22* and *69* in the present catalogue, came from the collection of the Leipzig publisher and connoisseur, Rudolph Weigel (d. 1877). Beyond this, nothing is known of the sources on which Crocker drew.

Upon Crocker's death, the collections he had formed remained in the possession of his widow, in the sumptuous house at Sacramento that Crocker had purchased in his last years from the pioneer banker, B. F. Hastings. The house and its contents were given by Mrs. Crocker to the City of Sacramento and the California Museum Association in 1885, and are the nucleus around which the E. B. Crocker Art Gallery has grown.

Another private collector who purchased on a large scale was the late Moore S. Achenbach (1878-1963). He settled in San Francisco in 1918 to operate a highly successful advertising agency. His education (he had attended the Philadelphia Art Academy) and his business interested him in reproductive engraving, and from this it was a short step to an interest in engraving in general and, by extension, in drawing. He began collecting prints and master drawings systematically in the 1930's, and before his death had assembled a collection of almost 100,000 prints and 750 drawings. In the latter category he bought single sheets, principally on the English and French markets, and he bought one collection *en bloc.* This was the early nineteenth-century collection formed by Joseph Green Cogswell, acquired by Mortimer L. Schiff of New York, and then bought entire by Achenbach in 1939. In 1949 he incorporated his possessions as the Achenbach Foundation for Graphic Arts. Since 1951 this Foundation has been housed in the California Palace of the Legion of Honor at San Francisco. An endowment has permitted both the print and drawing collections of the Foundation to continue to grow. The most notable addition to the

latter since Achenbach's death has been the Georges
de Batz Collection of eighteenth-century French and
Italian drawings, purchased in 1967.

Other drawing collections in California have been built
by bequests to institutions or by purchase campaigns. The
late Mortimer Leventritt, son of a San Francisco banking
family, from whom he inherited numerous art objects
and an interest in acquiring more, left a conspicuous
collection of oriental works of art and Venetian furniture,
paintings and drawings, to his *alma mater,* Stanford
University, in 1941. In this fashion the Tiepolos in the present
exhibition (catalogue numbers 54, 60, 61) came to
Stanford. A purchase fund has existed since that time for
enlarging the collection, and several significant purchases
have been made in recent times, among them the study
by Géricault (catalogue number 7).

The Santa Barbara Museum of Art was founded in 1941,
with an orientation toward American art. In the late
1950's, however, collecting was extended to the old masters,
and with the help of Santa Barbara collectors, chief
among whom is Wright Ludington, an important small
group of drawings was acquired, five of which figure
in the present exhibition.

The Art Division of The Los Angeles County Museum
acquired drawings for many years as a normal part of its
collecting, principally by way of gift, and in the field of
modern art. A separate department of prints and drawings
was set up after World War II, however. As funds became
available, systematic purchasing of old master drawings
was begun in the mid-1950's, and has been carried on
at an increasing rate to the present day.

Private collectors have continued to be active alongside
the new institutions. Norton Simon stands out especially
for having accumulated a considerable number of master
drawings for his own collection, for The Norton Simon
Foundation, and for the Hunt Foods & Industries Museum
of Art. He has lent extremely generously from all three
collections to this exhibition.

The continuing growth of the State's population and wealth,
and the national development of an increasing interest in
the fine arts, promise that this activity will continue
unabated into the future. Collectors, both private and
institutional, grumble about the impending end to
collecting, due to the scarcity of fine sheets and the soaring
saleroom prices. But, as can be seen from this exhibition,
which includes a significant number of drawings acquired
by their present owners in the last ten years, fine drawings
by major artists are still available to those patient and
persistent enough to seek them out. The University Art
Museum is itself admirably represented, having begun to
acquire drawings only in the past two years. We may hope
therefore that an exhibition such as this represents no more
than a foretaste of what future generations of Californians
will be able to see in the drawing cabinets of their State.

JUERGEN SCHULZ

29:106   DOMENICO BECCAFUMI   *Descent from the Cross*, ca. 1540

Major reference numbers in the catalogue entries section, example above, are to be interpreted as follows: 29 indicates the catalogue number assigned to the drawing *Descent from the Cross;* 106 indicates the page number on which the reproduction of the drawing appears.

The reference numbers in the plates section of the catalogue will appear at the bottom of the page as in the example below.

29:36   *Descent from the Cross*

---

106   DOMENICO BECCAFUMI (1486–1551)

---

29 indicates the catalogue number for *Descent from the Cross;* 36 indicates the page number on which the entry for the drawing appears.

INDICATIONS

Dimensions are given in millimeters; height precedes width. Paper color is white or off-white, except where indicated. Left and right are spectator's left and right unless otherwise indicated. Initials following the catalogue entries identify the compiler:

D.A./Don Ackland;   E.G./Elizabeth De Gall;

S.H./Sungmii Han;   S.K./Susan King;

C.M./Carolyn Malone;   L.O./Lynn Ostling;

M.Q./Mae Quan;   N.R./Natalie Rosenberg;

M.S./Marcus Sopher;   J.St./June Steingart;

E.S./Elizabeth Sullivan;   M.T./Michael Tepper;

K.T./Keith Thoreen;   D.T./Diane Turner;

Unsigned entries are by the editor of the catalogue.

BIBLIOGRAPHICAL ABBREVIATIONS

Bartsch, *Peintre graveur:* A. von Bartsch, *Le peintre graveur . . .* , 21 vols., Vienna, 1803-1821.

Hellman, *Original Drawings:* G. S. Hellman, *Original Drawings by the Old Masters: The Collection formed by Joseph Green Cogswell, 1786-1871*, New York, 1915.

Lugt: F. Lugt, *Les marques des collections de dessins & d'estampes; marques estampillées et écrites de collections particulières et publiques*, Amsterdam, 1921-1956.

Nagler, *Monogrammisten:* G. K. Nagler, *Die monogrammisten und diejenigen bekannten und unbekannten künstler aller schulen, welche sich zur bezeichnung ihrer werke eines figürlichen zeichens, der initialen des namens, der abbreviatur desselben, etc., bedient haben,* Munich, 1858-1879.

Tietzes, *Drawings:* H. Tietze and E. Tietze-Conrat, *The Drawings of the Venetian Painters in the Fifteenth and Sixteenth Centuries,* New York, 1944.

Vasari, *Vite:* G. Vasari, *Le vite de' più eccellenti pittori, scultori ed architettori,* vols. I-VII of Giorgio Vasari, *Le Opere di Giorgio Vasari* [con nuove annotazione e commenti di Gaetano Milanesi], Florence, 1878-1885.

Venturi, *Storia:* A. Venturi, *Storia dell' arte italiana . . .* , Milan, 1901-1940.

ARTISTS IN EXHIBITION

English FUSELI, HENRY
ROWLANDSON, THOMAS
WILKIE, SIR DAVID

French DELACROIX, EUGENE
FRAGONARD, JEAN HONORE
GERICAULT, THEODORE
GUERIN, FRANCOIS
INGRES, JEAN AUGUSTE DOMINIQUE
LANCRET, NICOLAS
MEISSONIER, ERNEST
PATEL, PIERRE, THE ELDER
QUESNEL, FRANCOIS
RIGAUD, HYACINTHE
SUBLEYRAS, PIERRE, STYLE OF
VAN LOO, CARLE
WATTEAU, ANTOINE

German CALCAR, JAN STEFAN VAN
CHODOWIECKI, DANIEL
MASTER OF THE MUHLDORF ALTAR
RUMOHR, KARL FRIEDRICH LUDWIG FELIX VON
ZICK, JANUARIUS

Italian BARBIERI, GIOVANNI FRANCESCO
BECCAFUMI, DOMENICO
BELLOTTO, BERNARDO
CANTAGALLINA, REMIGIO
CARPACCIO, VITTORE
CARRACCI, ANNIBALE
CHIMENTI, JACOPO
FARINATO, PAOLO
GHEZZI, PIER LEONE
GUARDI, FRANCESCO
GUARDI, FRANCESCO, CIRCLE OF
LANFRANCO, GIOVANNI
MATURINO DA FIRENZE
MAZZOLA, GIROLAMO FRANCESCO MARIA
NEGRETTI, JACOPO
PIPPI, GIULIO
PONTE, FRANCESCO DA
PORTA, GIUSEPPE DELLA
PRETI, MATTIA
RENI, GUIDO
RICCI, SEBASTIANO
SCHIAVONE, ANDREA
SIGNORELLI, LUCA
TIBALDI, PELLEGRINO
TIEPOLO, GIOVANNI BATTISTA
TIEPOLO, GIOVANNI DOMENICO
TURCHI, ALESSANDRO

Netherlandish BERCHEM, NICLAES
BOSCH, HIERONYMUS, FOLLOWER OF
BREENBERGH, BARTHOLOMEUS
BRUEGEL, PIETER, THE YOUNGER
GOLTZIUS, HENDRIK
HEEMSKERCK, MARTEN VAN
RUBENS, PETER PAUL
SAVERY, ROELANT
STRAET, JAN VAN DER
SWANEVELT, HERMAN VAN
VALCKENBORCH, FREDERICK VAN

SANTA BARBARA MUSEUM OF ART. Museum No. 61.71.
521 x 584 mm.; brush and dark and light grey wash
heightened with white.
Collections: Baroness North; Arthur Grossland; P. & D.
Colnaghi & Co., Ltd., London; Rosenbach Stock; John
Fleming; Zeitlin & Ver Brugge, Los Angeles. *Exhibited:*
Pomona College Art Gallery, Claremont, California, *The
Art of the Sublime,* 1964, cat. no. 21; University of Redlands,
Tom and Ann Peppers Art Center, Redlands, California,
Man's Spirit and the Visual Arts, 1967.

The drawing is one of several preparatory sketches for the
now-lost painting, *The Vision of the Madhouse,* from the
"Milton Gallery", a cycle of paintings by Fuseli illustrating
the works of Milton. The scene in the present case is from
Paradise Lost, XI, lines 477-485. In the center of the drawing
a raving man is trying to escape from a warder and from
a kneeling woman who holds his waist with her left arm.
Together with this central group many other frenzied figures
form a compact mass in the shallow stage-like space. At the
top of the picture an evil spirit with bat's wings, barely
visible in the darkness, overshadows the entire figure group.
Another drawing of exactly the same subject and of almost
identical composition is owned by the Kunsthaus in Zürich.[1]
In the latter, the entire upper area occupied by the demon
is strongly lighted and the figures in general show stronger
contrast of light and dark than in the Santa Barbara drawing.
The painting of this scene was completed in February, 1793,
while the whole cycle had been started in 1790.[2] Our
drawing can be dated therefore in the years 1790-1792.
Of the forty-seven paintings which constituted the cycle,
only twenty-five can be located today.

[1]No. 1916/10; P.Ganz, *The Drawings of Henry Fuseli,*
London, 1949, pl. 86; F.Antal, *Fuseli Studies,* London,
1956, pl. 26a. [2]G.Schiff, *Johann Heinrich Füsslis Milton-
Galerie,* Zürich, 1963, 150.   S.H.

THE LOS ANGELES COUNTY MUSEUM OF ART. Museum
No. 49.17.1.
457 x 358 mm.; slightly trimmed all around; pen and brown
ink and colored washes; signed, "Rowlandson. 1794" (lower
right).
Collections: William Randolph Hearst, Los Angeles.

Rowlandson was trained in the orthodox fashion of his day
at the Royal Academy Schools, London, where he studied

in the traditional academic manner, including drawing from plaster casts. There followed trips to France and the Netherlands, and the commencement of a career as a painter of serious subjects. Rowlandson's early landscapes, portraits and "subject pictures" were in character with and were exhibited alongside those of Romney, Gainsborough, Moreland and Reynolds. At the age of twenty-nine, however, he suddenly abandoned serious painting and turned to caricature and visual satire, a genre of painting which William Hogarth had already made popular earlier in the century.[1] Although Rowlandson became famous above all for his political cartoons and caricatures, it is his social satire that interests us most today. In his gentler scenes, such as this, he modeled himself clearly on the Dutch genre painters of the seventeenth century. But he was capable of more acid criticism as well, in which his models were Hogarth and the other satirists of his day.

Here two young maids flirt with some country lads who have stopped at the inn for their midday meal. One serves the beer, the other tastes the meal to make sure it is right. The only thing that mars this idyl is the innkeeper, who interrupts the tryst with a querulous mien from the window above.

[1] B.Falk, *Thomas Rowlandson, His Life and Art,* London and New York, 1949. S.K.

3:80   SIR DAVID WILKIE (1785-1841)   *The Arrival of the Rich Relation,* ca. 1810-1818

ACHENBACH FOUNDATION FOR GRAPHIC ARTS, CALIFORNIA PALACE OF THE LEGION OF HONOR, SAN FRANCISCO.
243 x 306 mm.; pen and brown ink.
Collections: Squire Gallery, London; Collis P. Huntington.
Literature: Portfolio, 1887, XVIII, opposite 92.

Wilkie was born at Cults, Fifeshire, the son of a minister. He showed an early artistic aptitude and began his studies to that end at the age of fourteen, in Edinburgh.
In 1805, at the age of nineteen, he entered the Royal Academy Schools in London, and a year later achieved his first success with *The Village Politicians.* This type of innocent genre painting with which he began his career remained the hallmark of his early years, until around 1818.[1] It was said that his ". . . poverty at this time saved him from italianizing through a Roman schooling."[2] Later trips abroad did away with the naive charm he exhibited in his early works.
His genre paintings of the years 1806-1818 were inspired in part by Dutch artists such as Ostade and Teniers.
Wilkie abstained from the grosser side of comedy found in Teniers, and preserved in his paintings a sometimes too-sweet innocence, which however is lacking in *The Arrival of the Rich Relation,* making it unusual among his early work. The drawing was probably a study for a picture, but no finished painting of the subject is known.[3]

[1]*The Art Union,* 1842, IV, 159-160, n. 11 (on *The Penny Wedding* of 1818). [2]*D.S.MacColl,* "Scottish Painters," *Burlington Magazine,* 1939, LXXIV, 4. [3]A chalk drawing of the same subject accompanied the present sheet when it was sold at Christie's in 1842; cf. *The Art Union, loc.cit.*   L.O.

4:81   EUGENE DELACROIX (1798–1863)   *Two Squatting Arabs*

PRIVATE COLLECTION, BEVERLY HILLS.
104 x 154 mm.; pencil and water color; stamped, "E D" (lower right).
Collections: Henri Cottereau, Paris. *Exhibited:* Volkswagenwerk, Wolfsburg, *Französische Malerei von Delacroix bis Picasso,* 1961, cat. no. 183 (illus.); Mills College Art Gallery, Oakland, California, *Drawings, Watercolors and Prints by Eugène Delacroix in West Coast Collections,* 1963, cat. no. 9 (illus.).

This drawing is one of many that Delacroix made during his voyage of 1832 to Morocco in the company of the Comte de Mornay. As in the *Petits Personnages* of 1832,[1] the background of *Two Squatting Arabs* is hardly indicated; the artist is interested exclusively in details of dress and physiognomy. The motive of seated Arabs is found in numerous sepia studies of 1832,[2] and a squatting figure similar to that in this drawing appears in Delacroix's etching of 1833, *Arabs of Oran.*[3] The impressions of the trip remained with the artist as late as 1855. In the *Arabes Voyageants* of that year the same exotic subject matter appears,[4] although these later paintings are no longer earthy records of village life, but brilliant pageants of oriental splendor.

[1]A.Sefrioui, *Delacroix au Maroc,* Rabat, 1963, pl. II. [2]A.Robaut and E.Chesneau, *L'Oeuvre complet de Eugène Delacroix, 1813-63,* Paris, 1885, nos. 439 ff. [3]E.Delacroix, *Journal,* ed. W.Pach, London, 1938, opposite 176. [4]Sefrioui, *op.cit.,* pl. IX.   D.T.

5:82   JEAN HONORE FRAGONARD (1732–1806)   *An Italian Park,* 1786

E. B. CROCKER ART GALLERY, SACRAMENTO. Museum No. 407-24.
240 x 370 mm.; laid down; pencil, pen and brown ink and wash; signed "Frago 1786" (on the stela, lower right).
Collections: Edwin Crocker, Sacramento.
Literature: A. Ananoff, *L'oeuvre dessiné de Jean Honoré*

Fragonard, Paris, 1961-1963, II, cat. no. 947. *Exhibited:*
E. B. Crocker Art Gallery, Sacramento, *Three Centuries of
Landscape Drawing,* 1940, cat. no. 63a; idem, *Drawings
of the Masters,* 1959; idem, *French Landscape Artists,* 1960.

The last representative of the rococo style in France,
Fragonard carried on the eighteenth-century tradition of
suggesting the ephemerality of life by presenting charming
little figures wandering through a picturesque setting of
ruins and antique statuary. He developed an interest
in outdoor scenes on his first trip to Italy, where he went on
sketching trips with Hubert Robert and the Abbé Saint-Non.
Among drawings originating from a second trip to Rome
in 1774, we find a park or cemetery sketch[1] which
Fragonard transformed, with only a few slight changes,
into a larger format twelve years later. The result is the
Crocker drawing of 1786, more sensitively delineated than
the earlier sketch from life. The wash technique of his
old age seems to dissolve the foliage into shimmering forms,
and subtle accents have been added which had not been
part of the original composition, such as the man with the
broad-brimmed hat resting in the foreground.

[1]Ananoff, *op.cit.,* cat. no. 946.   N.R.

6:83   JEAN HONORE FRAGONARD   *Danaë Visited by Jupiter*

COLLECTION MR. AND MRS. NORTON SIMON, LOS ANGELES.
270 x 394 mm.; pen and brown ink and wash.
Collections: Chabot and Duc de La Mure or Desmarets,
Paris; Vigée-Lebrun, Paris; Tripier-Lefranc, Paris;
Léon Decloux, Sèvres; Kraemer, Paris; Félix Doistau; David
Weill, Paris; Charles E. Slatkin Galleries, Inc., New York.
Literature: R. Portalis, *Fragonard,* 1889, 298 (illus.);
A. Dayot and L. Vaillat, *Chardin-Fragonard,* Paris, 1907,
pl. 155; G. Henriot, *Collection David Weill,* Paris, 1928, III,
123 (illus.); C. F. Foerster, *Jean-Honoré Fragonard,* Berlin,
n.d., pl. 25; A. Ananoff, *L'Oeuvre dessiné de Fragonard,*
Paris, 1961-1963, I, cat. no. 394 (illus.), II (Corrigenda),
309. *Exhibited:* Musée du Grand Palais, Paris,
Chardin-Fragonard, 1907, cat. no. 171; Pavillon de Marson,
Paris, *Fragonard,* 1921, cat. no. 165.

Danaë, the daughter of Acrisius, was visited by the
god Jupiter in the form of a shower of gold. Jupiter's eagle
appears in the upper right, and a heap of golden coins
lies all about Danaë, who is still held in the embrace of the
divine cloud. The excitement of the scene is enhanced by
the spots of intense highlighting which flicker horizontally
across the sheet as well as by the fluttering movement
of such details as the garment of the maid with the jug,
and the jet of water.
An earlier and unfinished version of the composition exists.[1]
All the elements are the same, except for the figure of
Danaë who, instead of gazing toward the eagle, turns her

face away from the cloud and downward. The difference is striking. On the one hand, Danaë's rejection of the god is implied; on the other, an imbalance is created within the composition by the invitation to look to the left, away from the central action. In the present drawing the psychological and formal unity of the scene is complete. The degree of finish, which is greater than in the majority of Fragonard's sketches, suggests that the drawing may have been a preparatory sketch for a painting. No painting of the subject is known to have existed, however, besides a now-lost canvas based on Rembrandt's *Danaë*.[2]

[1]A.Ananoff, *op.cit.,* I, cat. no. 393 (illus.). [2]G.Wildenstein, *Fragonard,* Aylesbury, 1960, cat. no. 3.   S.K.

7:84   THEODORE GERICAULT (1791–1824)   *Eight Male Nudes*

STANFORD UNIVERSITY MUSEUM.
204 x 231 mm.; pencil.
Collections: Eugène Dévéria, Paris;[1] Seiferheld Galleries, New York.
Literature: Facsimile de dessins extraits des livres de croquis de Géricault et lithographiés par plusieurs artistes, Paris, 1825, pl. 15.

The drawing is a free transposition of motives from the *Small Last Judgment* by Rubens, now in the Alte Pinakothek at Munich.[2] Traditionally it has been called a study for a *Last Judgment,* but Géricault is not known to have undertaken such a composition, and—as has been pointed out by Professor Lorenz Eitner—some of the figures reappear in the preparatory studies which Géricault made for his most famous work, *The Raft of the Medusa,* in the Louvre.[3]
In two studies for the rebelling sailors of the *Raft,* now in the Gemeente Museum, Amsterdam, and the Fogg Art Museum, Cambridge,[4] Géricault introduced figures resembling the center and lower left figures of the present drawing. The conception of a loose mass of falling bodies sprawling over each other and swarming outward is also similar.
During his visit to Italy in 1816-1817 Géricault copied large parts of Michelangelo's *Last Judgment* in the Sistine Chapel, which had been the inspiration in turn also to Rubens. The fact that the present drawing is based on a *Last Judgment* by Rubens and recalls more generally the fresco of Michelangelo seems not insignificant. Clearly, Géricault was trying to give to his subject of a modern, secular disaster the meaning of a profound and broader tragedy.[5]

[1]C.Clément, *Géricault,* Paris, 1879, 420, no. 15. [2]Clément, *loc.cit.* [3]Information generously provided by Professor Eitner, who is soon to publish the drawing. [4]K.Berger, *Géricault,* Vienna, 1952, pls. 46, 47. [5]Cf. L.Eitner,

Géricault, unpublished Ph.D. dissertation, Princeton
University, 1951.   D.T.

8:85   FRANCOIS GUERIN (BEFORE 1751–AFTER 1791)   *Madame de Pompadour with her Daughter,*
Alexandrine d'Etiolles, before 1754

E. B. CROCKER ART GALLERY, SACRAMENTO. Museum
No. 403-5.
235 x 190 mm.; laid down; red, white and black chalk on
blue paper.
Collections: Edwin Crocker, Sacramento.
Literature: M. N. Benisovich, "A Bust of Alexandrine
d'Etiolles by Saly," *Gazette des Beaux Arts,* 6e Pér., 1945,
XXVIII, 31-42 (illus.); O. Benesch, "Two Drawings
dedicated to Mme. de Pompadour," *Gazette des Beaux Arts,*
6e Pér., 1950, XXXVII, 125-129 (illus.). *Exhibited:* E. B.
Crocker Art Gallery, Sacramento, *Drawings of the
Masters,* 1959.

Guérin began his career in 1751 as a student of Natoire,
a professor in the Académie de Saint-Luc at Paris, and
by 1765 had been accepted in the Académie Royale.
His position in the circle of Mme. de Pompadour was a
minor one compared with that of Boucher, and it is the
latter to whom the Sacramento drawing has been attributed
in the past. The true author was recognized in 1945 by
Michel Benisovich, who connected the study with a painting
by Guérin in the collection of Baron Edmund de Rothschild
at Paris.[1] The painting reverses the composition and
replaces the *amoretti* and allegorical setting with a domestic
interior. The pose of Mme. de Pompadour has become
more erect, and her hands are shown stroking a small dog
and holding a book, but all the essential elements of the
drawing reappear in the painting.
A lost painting by Boucher, last heard of in a sale of 1881,
corresponds perfectly in the description with the painting
and drawing of Guérin.[2] It seems very likely, therefore, that
the latter derived his composition from the more
famous artist.
The attribution to Guérin of the painting has an excellent
pedigree. The inventory of 1781 of the collection of
Mme. de Pompadour's heir, the Marquis de Marigny, lists
the picture as a work of Guérin, along with two other
paintings now lost but recognizable in drawings that
survive in the Albertina.[3] The style of the latter agrees
with that of the Sacramento study.[4]
The Marquis de Marigny also owned a drawing by Boucher,
dated 1754, now in the National Gallery of Victoria,
Melbourne, of Mme. de Pompadour surrounded by a
garland of flowers carried by three *amoretti* who surmount
symbols of the arts, among which is the overturned
bust of a young girl.[5] This poignant and lovely drawing
symbolizes the death of the ten-year-old Alexandrine
in 1754. Representations of Mme. de Pompadour and her
beloved daughter are rare; aside from Guérin's painting and
drawing and Boucher's now lost grisaille, we know of

only a miniature by Baudoin.[6] Although our drawing is perhaps not from life, it is unlikely that it would have been done after 1754.

[1]Benisovich, *loc.cit.* [2]Lot 13 in the Bourneville sale of 1881; cf. Benisovich, *op.cit.,* 36. [3]Respectively, nos. 45 and 46a-b in the inventory; E.Campardon, *Mme. de Pompadour,* Paris, 1863, 331 ff. The drawings were published by Benesch, *loc.cit.* [4]A signed and dated drawing of 1752 by Guérin, in the Louvre, agrees as well; Musée du Louvre et Musée de Versailles, Paris, *Inventaire générale des dessins de l'école française,* 1907-1921, VI, cat. no. 4636 (illus.). [5]Inv. no. 283; Campardon, *loc.cit.;* cf. R.Schoolman and C.Slatkin in Master Drawings, 1967, V, 64 (illus.). [6]Benisovich, *op.cit.,* 34-36.   D.A.

9:88   JEAN AUGUSTE DOMINIQUE INGRES (1780–1867)   *Scipio and his Son with the Envoys of Antiochus,* ca. 1800

HUNT FOODS & INDUSTRIES MUSEUM OF ART, FULLERTON.
242 x 373 mm.; pencil and grey wash; signed lower left, "jngres inv.int."
Collections: Hanns Schaeffer Galleries, Los Angeles.
Exhibited: Fogg Art Museum, Cambridge, *Ingres Centennial Exhibition,* 1967.

The drawing is a finished composition study for the painting of *Scipio and his Son with the Envoys of Antiochus,* submitted by Ingres in 1800 for the Prix de Rome of the Académie des Beaux-Arts, and awarded the second Grand Prix. The set subject of the competition was the story of the generosity of Antiochus the Great, King of Syria: "Antiochus, informed that Scipio lay ill in Helle, sent him his son, who had been taken prisoner, that joy might cure the disease of the body. After holding his son for a long time in his embrace, Scipio said to the Envoys of Antiochus, 'go and offer the King my grateful thanks'."[1] The painting was later in the collection of Edouard Gatteaux and was destroyed by fire in 1871. It has usually been called *Antiochus and the Ambassadors* or *Antiochus and Scipio,* although the King himself does not appear in it. A more accurate title is the one used here. The sheet is an important early drawing by Ingres, done during the time he was in the studio of David. Another drawing of the same period repeats almost exactly the figure of Scipio in the present composition.[2]

[1]G.Wildenstein, *Ingres,* London, n. d., cat. no. 2, with further references. [2]Musée Ingres, Montauban, *Peintures: Ingres et son temps (artistes nés entre 1740-1830),* Paris, 1965, cat. no. 147: *Torso of a Man,* ca. 1800, made in David's studio.   J.St.

COLLECTION MR. AND MRS. NORTON SIMON, LOS ANGELES.
203 x 159 mm.; folded on all sides; pencil.
Literature: M. Tinti, *Lorenzo Bartolini,* Rome, 1936, 80-81;
H. Naef, "Ingres als Portraitist im Elternhause Bartolinis,"
Paragone, 1956, VII, lxxxiii, 31-38 (illus.).

11:86   JEAN AUGUSTE DOMINIQUE INGRES   *Maria Maglia Bartolini,* 1806

COLLECTION MR. AND MRS. NORTON SIMON, LOS ANGELES.
210 x 152 mm.; folded on all sides; pencil.
Literature: M. Tinti, *Lorenzo Bartolini,* Rome, 1936, 80-81;
H. Naef, "Ingres als Portraitist im Elternhause Bartolinis,"
Paragone, 1956, VII, lxxxiii, 31-38 (illus.).

Liborio and Maria Bartolini were the parents of the
sculptor Lorenzo Bartolini, whom Ingres met and befriended
in the Paris studio of David where they were both pupils.
The drawings are two of a set of four, the others
representing two brothers of Lorenzo (now also in the
collection of Mr. and Mrs. Norton Simon).
When first published the four drawings were dated to
Ingres' stay in Florence of 1820-1824.[1] More recently, Hans
Naef has suggested they were made during Ingres' short
stay at the Bartolini house, 2-9 October, 1806, when he was
on his way to Rome.[2] This would place them at the very
beginning of the artist's first Italian period.
Letters by Ingres to Gilbert of June, 1821 and October, 1823
show that by that time the painter and the Bartolini
were no longer on good terms, and it seems unlikely that
Ingres would have portrayed them at that time. Also,
the ages of the sitters accord better with an early date:
in 1806 the elder Bartolini was 62, the mother 55. By the
1820's Liborio had been dead for some time and Maria
was in her seventies.
Stylistically the portrait of Bartolini's father is akin to
other drawings by Ingres of 1806, such as the drawing of the
Forestier family in the Louvre,[3] and the portrait of
Naudet, the landscape painter and draughtsman, in the
Fogg Art Museum.[4] It has the dainty touch and simplicity
of the early drawings, not the relatively broad and free
manner of the 1820's.

[1]Tinti, *loc.cit.* [2]Naef, *loc.cit.* [3]G.Wildenstein, *Ingres,*
London, 1954, 23. [4]Fogg Art Museum, Cambridge, *Ingres
Centennial Exhibition,* 1967, cat. no. 6.   A.Q.

ACHENBACH FOUNDATION FOR GRAPHIC ARTS, CALIFORNIA PALACE OF THE LEGION OF HONOR, SAN FRANCISCO. 206 x 129 mm.; red chalk; inscribed in various modern hands, "WPK" (center, verso), "D 315, 4705", "Vente: Jacques Doucet 1905" and "figure pour l'hiver" (bottom, verso).
Collections: William Pitcairn Knowles, Rotterdam (Lugt 2643); Jacques Doucet; Schaeffer Galleries, New York.
Exhibited: The Baltimore Museum of Art, *The Age of Elegance,* 1959, cat. no. 60.

The figure appears to be a study for a larger composition, but its counterpart has not been found in Lancret's known paintings. There is some similarity to the skater bending down to help a lady get up from the ice in the painting of *L'Hiver,* one of four paintings of the seasons executed by Lancret in 1738 for the Château de la Mouette.[1] It is known that Lancret entered the studio of Watteau's master, Claude Gillot, in 1712-1717, and that he met and was profoundly influenced by Watteau himself.[2] The influence of both men can be seen in the Achenbach drawing. The elongation of the figure and the small head recall Gillot's style. One may compare the figures in Gillot's pen and wash drawing of *Four Comedians,* and in his pen and red chalk drawing of *A Scene in the Theatre,* both in the Louvre.[3] The handling of the red chalk medium, on the other hand, resembles Watteau's drawing of *A Turbaned Persian* (no. *21* in the present catalogue), which represents Watteau's mature style. Lancret's line is more schematic than Watteau's, but he obtains an effect of rapidity and spontaneity that is entirely his own.

[1] G.Wildenstein, *Nicolas Lancret,* Paris, 1924, 71, fig. 13.
[2] Cf. J.W.McCoubrey in the *Encyclopedia of World Art,* London and New York, 1959-1967, VIII, s.v. Lancret.
[3] J.Mathey, "Drawings by Watteau and Gillot," *Burlington Magazine,* 1960, CII, 354-361, figs. 17, 19.   S.H.

13:90   ERNEST MEISSONIER (1815–1891)   *The Chessplayer*

M. H. DE YOUNG MEMORIAL MUSEUM, SAN FRANCISCO (ON EXTENDED LOAN TO THE ACHENBACH FOUNDATION FOR GRAPHIC ARTS, CALIFORNIA PALACE OF THE LEGION OF HONOR, SAN FRANCISCO).
218 x 173 mm.; pencil; signed with the artist's monogram (lower left),[1] inscribed, "55.5" (upper left, verso).
Collections: Unidentified (blind stamp, "B O" in an oval, bottom right, recto); H. Giacomelli, Paris;[2] Mrs. Andre Arogan, San Francisco.

The literalism and control of this drawing are characteristic of Meissonier's middle years. One may compare his study of an *Evangelist* of 1838, or the study for his Salon painting of *A Sunday at Poissy,* exhibited in 1850.[3] In both, Meissonier reproduces with the same dryness the light and shadow effects of pulled or folded cloth, seeking to capture its materiality. The same care is taken with details, such as the glistening buttons on the costume and even the row of nails which fastens the upholstery to the frame of the cabriole chair. Earlier drawings are more freely executed and use a livelier, more staccato line.[4] Later Meissonier's style grew less explicit.[5]

There is record of three paintings of chess players by the artist, but the figure is not known to be related directly to any of them.

[1]Nagler, *Monogrammisten,* II, no. 1679. [2]Sold, Hôtel Drouot, Paris, 13-15 April, 1905, lot 210. [3]V.Gréard, *Meissonier,* New York, 1897, respectively opposite 286, 278. [4]*Ibid.,* 45. [5]*Ibid.,* 297.   D.T.

14:91   PIERRE PATEL THE ELDER (CA. 1620–1676)   recto: *Landscape with Ruins,* ca. 1650–1652
verso: *Landscape with Rural Buildings*

E. B. CROCKER ART GALLERY, SACRAMENTO. Museum No. 394-12.
150 x 227 mm.; cut on all sides, vertical tears; black chalk heightened with white on grey paper (recto), pen and brown ink and grey wash (verso).
Collections: Edwin Crocker, Sacramento. *Exhibited:* E. B. Crocker Art Gallery, Sacramento, *Three Centuries of Landscape Drawing,* 1941, cat no. 58; *idem, French Landscape Artists,* 1960.

Patel was a student of Vouet and functioned in the latter's studio as a specialist in landscape. He was a member of the Académie de Saint-Luc in 1635; executed a series of landscapes for the decoration of the Cabinet de l'Amour at the Hôtel Lambert in ca. 1646-1647, where La Hire, Le Brun and Le Sueur also worked; and collaborated in ca. 1655 with Romanelli in the decoration of the apartment of Queen Anne of Austria at the Louvre.

Today works by Patel are not so plentiful or popular as they were in the eighteenth century, at which time he enjoyed a reputation as the "Claude Lorrain of France."[1] Patel's landscapes are all very similar, but no painting exists that corresponds exactly with the present drawing. The nearest work is a *Landscape with the Journey to Emmaus,* dated 1652, in the collection of Walter P. Chrysler, Jr., which differs only in a few minor details and in the disposition of the figures.[2]

A somewhat less finished landscape drawing in black chalk by Patel, in the Ecole des Beaux-Arts, shows the same composition in reverse.[3] It is a study for the undated *Landscape with a Goatherd* in the Musée des Beaux-Arts at Orléans.[4]

The differences between the Crocker drawing and the related painting and drawing give insight into Patel's working method and ideas. Landscape is a pre-established setting into which various themes or genre figures can be introduced without significantly changing the elegiac sentiment evoked by the Italian landscape and ruins. Changes are primarily concerned with details of architecture, the degree of balance between left and right, and the interplay of foliage and architecture. But the mood and, in a sense, the content, remain the same.

The study on the verso, which is cruder in style and hastier in execution than the recto, must be by a different hand than Patel's, and may have been the exercise of a pupil in his studio.

[1] P.J.Mariette, in the *Abécédario;* P.de Chennevières and A.de Montaiglon, *L'Abécédario de Mariette...,* Paris *(Archives de l'Art Française),* 1851-1856, IV, 88-90, 857-858. [2] Exhibited, The Finch College Museum of Art, New York, *Vouet to Rigaud,* 1967, cat. no. 28 (illus.). [3] No. 34630, signed; J.Vallery-Radot, *Le dessin français au XVII siècle,* Lausanne, 1953, 197, no. 115 (illus.). [4] J.Thuillier and A.Châtelet, *French Painting from Le Nain to Fragonard,* Geneva, 1964, pl. 57.   D.A.

15:92   FRANCOIS QUESNEL (1543/1544-1619)   *Portrait of a Nobleman*

THE NORTON SIMON FOUNDATION, FULLERTON (ON EXTENDED LOAN TO THE LOS ANGELES COUNTY MUSEUM OF ART). 270 x 203 mm.; trimmed slightly all around; pencil and red chalk; dated 1589 (top right).
Collections: Henri du Bouchet de Bournonville de Villeflix; Jacques du Bouchet de Villeflix; Charles Wickert, Paris; Edward M. Hodges, Paris.
Literature: L. Delteil, *Catalogue des crayons français du XVIe siècle composant la collection de M. Charles Wickert,* Paris, 1909, cat. no. 30; L. Dimier, *Histoire de la peinture de portrait en France au XVIe siècle,* Paris, 1924-1925, I, pl. 53, II, 236; E. Moreau-Nélaton, *Les Clouets et leurs émules,* Paris, 1924, I, 99-100, II, 152-153. *Exhibited:* Cummer Gallery of Art, Jacksonville, Florida, *Loan Exhibition of Sixteenth Century French Art,* 1964.

The drawing closely resembles a group of pencil portraits in the Bibliothèque Nationale, a large part of which originated in the seventeenth-century collection of the de Villeflix.[1] Dimier and Moreau-Nélaton attribute this group to François Quesnel on the basis of similarities with a signed portrait of Henriette d'Entragues.[2] Quesnel's style corresponds with a later phase of French sixteenth-century portraiture, when the extreme naturalism of Clouet had become stylized to the point that the luster and delicacy of modeling he had given to the face had become flattened and dry. These later portraits remain historical documents, however, which record the tastes of French society of the time.

[1]E.Bonnaffé, *Dictionnaire des amateurs française au XVII siècle,* Paris, 1884, 323. Villeflix, Vileflix or V$_x$ appear on the back of many of the drawings in the group. [2]Dimier, *op.cit.,* 158; Moreau-Nélaton, *op.cit.,* 37.   M.T.

16:93   HYACINTHE RIGAUD (1659–1743)   *Study of Hands and Drapery,* 1735

Achenbach Foundation for Graphic Arts, California Palace of the Legion of Honor, San Francisco. Gift of Mr. and Mrs. Sidney M. Ehrman. Museum No. 1953.34. 295 x 451 mm.; black and white chalk on blue paper.
Collections: Pierre Cailleux, Paris.
Literature: A. Mongan, "A Drawing by Rigaud," *Bulletin of the California Palace of the Legion of Honor,* February, 1954, XI, no. 10; California Palace of the Legion of Honor, San Francisco, *Handbook of the Collections,* 1960, 56 (illus.). *Exhibited:* William Rockhill Nelson Gallery, Kansas City, Missouri, *The Century of Mozart,* 1956, cat. no. 14 (illus.); University Art Gallery, University of Minnesota, Minneapolis, *The Eighteenth Century—One Hundred Drawings by One Hundred Artists,* 1961, cat. no. 78; The John and Mable Ringling Museum of Art, Sarasota, Florida, *Master Drawings,* 1967.

As official court portraitist for Louis XIV, Rigaud with the aid of a large workshop produced an enormous number of portraits. One of the few that is entirely by his own hand is the portrait of 1735 of Gaspard de Gueidan, president of the Parliament of Provence, now in the Musée des Beaux-Arts at Aix-en-Provence. Gueidan is shown playing the *musette* or bagpipes, and the hands in the Achenbach drawing are the preparatory study for this pose. The drapery cannot be connected with any extant work by Rigaud. Such polished studies of hands and draperies were common in Rigaud's production, since the artist found it necessary to study every detail of his paintings from life, a method which Thuillier calls ". . . a pedantic concern for careful finish."[1] The artist stressed contour with fine gradations in shading, unlike many of his contemporaries who sought a more spontaneous effect with chalk.

[1]J.Thuillier and A.Châtelet, *French Painting from Le Nain to Fragonard,* Geneva, 1964, 136, quoting from Dézallier D'Argenville.   N.R.

17:94   PIERRE SUBLEYRAS (1699–1749), style of   *Saint Bernard of Clairvaux*

E. B. Crocker Art Gallery, Sacramento. Museum No. 303-12.

221 x 183 mm.; brown wash heightened with white, over stylus preparation, on dark brown paper; inscribed in an eighteenth-century hand, "N 427 . . . Ludwyk Carats" (verso).

Collections: Edwin Crocker, Sacramento. *Exhibited:* E. B. Crocker Art Gallery, Sacramento, *Drawings of the Masters,* 1959.

Wrongly attributed by a former owner to Ludovico Carracci, this enigmatic drawing reflects the hand of an eighteenth-century French master working in an Italianate style. The crisp draperies fall into folds that emphasize depth and recall the work of Subleyras, but in the opinion of an expert the drawing is not by him (written opinion of Pierre Rosenberg). The history painter Brenet has also been suggested, but other minor artists of the period had a drawing style similar to that of Brenet and Subleyras[1] and the attribution remains uncertain. The white habit with large capuche and ample sleeves can be securely identified as the costume of the Italian branch of the Bernardines or *Feuillants,* the reformed Cistercian order established at the end of the sixteenth century.[2] The presence of books and a pen most likely refers to Saint Bernard of Clairvaux, founder of the Cistercian order, although a halo is lacking.

The monumental pose of the figure might indicate that it was designed for a decorative mural scheme, but the figure itself is small. Since the reformed Cistercians possessed two monasteries in Rome and several houses throughout Italy, it is possible that the Crocker drawing stems from a chapel decoration in one of these buildings. The incision marks along the contours of the drawing suggest that it was either transferred onto another surface or copied from a previous design.

[1] Information kindly communicated by Anthony Clark.
[2] P. Helyot, *Histoire des ordres monastiques,* Paris, 1718, V, ch.38.   N.R.

18:95   CARLE VAN LOO (1705–1765)   *Standing Female Figure and Head of a Woman*

ACHENBACH FOUNDATION FOR GRAPHIC ARTS, CALIFORNIA PALACE OF THE LEGION OF HONOR, SAN FRANCISCO. 242 x 181 mm.; laid down; red, black and white chalk on blue paper; inscribed in a modern hand, "C. Van Loo" (verso). *Collections:* Joseph Green Cogswell; Mortimer L. Schiff; Moore S. Achenbach, San Francisco. *Literature:* Hellman, *Original Drawings,* cat. no. 231 (illus.).

Van Loo's training involved several years of study in Italy, and most likely the Achenbach drawing comes from his second Italian sojourn, 1724–1732. The draped female figure is handled with the same soft touch found in his preparatory study of *Diana* at The Metropolitan Museum of Art, New York, for frescoes in the Palazzo Stupinigi, Turin. However, it seems less a preparation for a painting than a classical figure exercise in the Italian manner. It is an attempt to coordinate the graceful flowing lines of a moving figure and to show the effect of the passions on the human physiognomy (in the detail at the right). Van Loo's difficulties with anatomical rendering are evident in the awkwardly drawn shoulders and the incorrect balancing of the figure's weight. Aware of his problems with figures in motion, Van Loo usually chose to diminish action in his paintings.   N.R.

19:97   ANTOINE WATTEAU (1684–1721)   *An Actor,* 1703–1707/1708

HUNT FOODS & INDUSTRIES MUSEUM OF ART, FULLERTON.
270 x 180 mm.; red chalk.
Collections: Lucien Guiraud.
Literature: K. T. Parker and J. Mathey, *Antoine Watteau: catalogue complet de son oeuvre dessiné,* Paris, 1957, I, cat. no. 72.

20:96   ANTOINE WATTEAU   *An Actress Dressed as Folly,* 1703–1707/1708

HUNT FOODS & INDUSTRIES MUSEUM OF ART, FULLERTON.
210 x 295 mm.; red chalk.
Collections: H.R.H. Elizabeth II, London.
Literature: Parker and Mathey, *op.cit.,* cat. no. 71.

It is most likely that these drawings were executed by Watteau in 1703-1707/1708, when he was studying with Claude Gillot in Paris. Gillot was very much attracted to the theater and was known for his depiction of subjects from the Italian *Commedia dell'arte,* an interest that Watteau inherited from him.[1] The identities of the persons represented in the present drawings are unknown. They do not seem to be members of an Italian troupe. The actor recalls one of the four dancers in Watteau's *Le Rêve de l'Artiste,* in the collection of David Weill at Paris, but is not identical.[2] According to Caylus, who spoke on Watteau's art before the Academy in 1748, it was the artist's habit to collect sketches for future use and refer back to them when making his compositions.[3] These figures may have been drawn for similar reference purposes.
The style of both drawings is that of Watteau's early period. The figures are similar to figures depicted by Gillot, such as those in his drawings of *Four Comedians* and of *A Scene in the Theatre,* both in the Louvre.[4] Almost all of Watteau's drawings are undated.[5] His drawings of Persians can be dated to 1715, because the Persian ambassador visited Paris in that year.[6] A comparison with one of the drawings of that party (no. *21* in the present catalogue) shows that the

present pair of studies is less mature. The chalk is applied to the paper relatively carefully and laboriously, and the hatching is relatively open and timid. The face, hand and pose are more expressive. Therefore, the drawing of the actor probably belongs to 1703-1707/1708 when Watteau was studying with Gillot.

[1]H.Adhemar, in *Encyclopedia of World Art,* London and New York, 1959-1967, s.v. Watteau; J.Thuillier and A.Châtelet, *French Painting from Le Nain to Fragonard,* Geneva, 1964, 158-164. [2]Parker and Mathey, *op.cit.,* I, 4, 11. [3]*Ibid.,* 15. [4]J.Mathey, "Drawings by Watteau and Gillot," *Burlington Magazine,* 1960, CII, 354-361, figs. 17, 19. [5]K.T.Parker, *The Drawings of Antoine Watteau,* London, 1930, 14. [6]Parker and Mathey, *op.cit.,* II, 349.   M.T.

21:98   ANTOINE WATTEAU   *A Turbaned Persian,* 1715

SAN FRANCISCO MUSEUM OF ART (ON EXTENDED LOAN TO THE ACHENBACH FOUNDATION FOR GRAPHIC ARTS, CALIFORNIA PALACE OF THE LEGION OF HONOR, SAN FRANCISCO).
427 x 236 mm.; red, black and white chalk on grey paper.
Collections: Flury-Hérard, Paris (Lugt 1015); Marquis de Chennoières, Paris (Lugt 2073); Henri Michel-Lévy; Charles Templeton Crocker, San Francisco.
Literature: K. T. Parker and J. Mathey, *Antoine Watteau: catalogue complet de son oeuvre dessiné,* Paris, 1957, II, cat. no. 797. *Exhibited:* Mills College Art Gallery, Oakland, California, *Old Master Drawings,* 1937; Portland Art Museum, Portland, Oregon, *Old Master Drawings,* 1938.

Eleven drawings of orientals are known in Watteau's oeuvre, although none appear in the artist's paintings. Jacques Mathey has shown that they can be traced to the year 1715 when the Persian ambassador arrived in Paris with a large suite.[1] Our drawing of the turbaned easterner is quite similar in facial character and dress, especially in the turban, to another drawing by Watteau of a seated Persian.[2] An attempt has been made to identify the subject as the ambassador himself, but a contemporary engraving of the Persian delegation arriving at the royal palace shows the entire entourage arrayed in similar costumes and turbans.[3] Furthermore, contemporary engravings of the ambassador, Mohammed Riza Bey, show recognizably different features. We may conclude, therefore, that it was not the portrait of a particular individual Watteau wished to record, but an exotic costume.

[1]J.Mathey, "Remarques sur la chronologie des peintures et dessins d'Antoine Watteau," *Bulletin de la Société d'Histoire de l'Art Française,* 1939, 158. [2]Parker and Mathey, *op.cit.,* II, cat. no. 790. [3]Mathey, "Remarques," 159.   M.T.

E. B. CROCKER ART GALLERY, SACRAMENTO. Museum
No. 127-21.
292 x 188 mm.; horizontal fold; red chalk; signed
(indistinctly) with the artist's monogram (lower right),[1]
inscribed in a later hand, "Jan van Kalkar" (bottom center).
Collections: Baron von Amstetter, Breslau; Rudolph Weigel,
Leipzig; Edwin Crocker, Sacramento.
Literature: L. Choulant, *Geschichte und Bibliographie der
anatomischen Abbildung,* Leipzig, 1852, 179, no. 43 (illus.
opposite 42); *idem, The History and Bibliography of
Anatomic Illustration,* trans. by M. Frank, Chicago, 1920,
417 (illus. 168).

The fame of the Flemish-born artist, Jan Stefan van Calcar,
rests primarily on his activity as an anatomical illustrator.
He was trained in Flanders, but moved to Venice in 1536
or 1537. There he became a follower of Titian, and it is
reputed that he learned to duplicate Titian's painting style.
There too, he became associated with the famous Belgian
anatomist, Andreas Vesalius (1514-1564). Between 1537
and 1543 he executed the bulk of the woodcut illustrations
for Vesalius' trial publication of 1538 for his monumental
treatise of 1543 on the human body and for the abridgment
of the latter published contemporaneously with new
illustrations. They are the first anatomical works based on a
close study of the human frame itself, rather than on
classical and medieval lore or on dissections of apes and
other animals.[2]
There is no direct correspondence between any of the
woodcuts from Vesalius' publications and the present
drawing. But it is very close in style to the woodcuts and
thus must date, like them, from the period 1537-1543. The
drawing was published in a facsimile woodcut by Kretschmar
in 1852, when in the possession of the Leipzig publisher and
collector Rudolph Weigel.[3] By 1920, however, it was
regarded as lost.[4] It was not among the items that figured
in the Weigel sales of 1870 and thus must have been disposed
of privately before that time.

[1]Nagler, *Monogrammisten,* IV, no. 743. [2]A.Vesalius, *Tabulae
anatomicae sex,* Venice, 1538; *De humani corporis fabricae
libri septem,* Basel, 1543; and *De humanis corporis fabricae
librorum epitome,* Basel, 1543. The first three of the six plates
in the *Tabulae* are by a different hand than Calcar's, and have
been attributed to Vesalius himself; J.B.deC.M.Saunders and
C.D.O'Malley, *The Illustrations from the Works of Andreas
Vesalius of Brussels,* Cleveland, 1950, 233-235. The other
three plates and all of the plates of the *Fabrica* and *Epitome*
are by Calcar according to the testimony of Vesalius himself.
[3]Choulant, *loc.cit.* [4]Choulant, trans. Frank, *loc.cit.*   S.K.

23:100   DANIEL CHODOWIECKI (1726–1801)   recto: *The Improvement of Morals*, ca. 1786
                                                  verso: *Figure Sketches*

E. B. CROCKER ART GALLERY, SACRAMENTO. Museum
No. 72-26.
202 x 336 mm.; red chalk and pencil, pen and black ink
(recto), black chalk (verso).
Exhibited: E. B. Crocker Art Gallery, Sacramento, *Old
Master Drawings from the E. B. Crocker Collection: The
German Masters, 15th to 19th Centuries,* 1939, cat. no. 14.

The drawing which has gone under the title of *The
Mountebank* is the finished study for an engraving of 1787
by Chodowiecki, entitled *Die Verbesserung der Sitten
(The Improvement of Morals).*[1]
Chodowiecki is best known as an engraver who reproduced
the small details of daily life in eighteenth-century Berlin.
Some of his prints, like *The Improvement of Morals,* reveal
a high degree of wit. The subject of the print is known from
a letter by the artist of 1787,[2] in which he mentions it in
regard to the plan of a competitor, the engraver Merino,
to publish an engraving each week of "the most interesting
events in Berlin." Merino's project collapsed after the
thirteenth week.
In this drawing Chodowiecki characterizes Merino as an
open-air orator with violin accompaniment whose lecture
on his thirteen engravings appeals mostly to children and
hysterical women. The title of the drawing and those titles
of Merino's engravings which are discernible from the
drawing—"Christmas Night," "The Wedding," "The
Concert," "The Theater," "The Quarrel," "The Robbery,"
"Sickness"—suggest that Merino's work had a trite, didactic
and moralistic tone, which particularly attracted
Chodowiecki's satire. Merino's claim to depict "interesting
events" is likewise satirized: while the crowd stands
enthralled at the commonplace events upon which Merino
expounds, a burning balloon, a cry from a second-story
window, a hanged man, an acrobat and a stiltwalker all
go unnoticed.

[1] W. Engelmann, *Daniel Chodowieckis sämmtliche
Kupferstiche,* Leipzig, 1857, 302, no. 572, and *idem, Archiv
für die Zeichnenden, Künste,* 1859, V, 254. [2] Ed. C.
Steinbrucker, *Briefe Daniel Chodowieckis an Anton Graff,*
Berlin and Leipzig, 1921, letter for 3 March 1787.   C.M.

24:102   MASTER OF THE MUHLDORF ALTAR (ACTIVE CA. 1505–CA. 1520)   *Annunciation,* 1514

E. B. CROCKER ART GALLERY, SACRAMENTO. Museum
No. 11-7.
207 x 150 mm.; slightly trimmed all around, laid down; pen
and black ink and wash heightened with white, on red
prepared paper; signed with the artist's monogram,[1] and
dated 1514.

Collections: Count Franz Joseph Sternberg, Prague; Edwin Crocker, Sacramento. *Exhibited:* E. B. Crocker Art Gallery, Sacramento, *Old Master Drawings from the E. B. Crocker Collection: The German Masters, 15th to 19th Centuries,* 1939, cat. no. 11; San Francisco International Exposition, Palace of Fine Arts, *Master Drawings,* 1940, cat. no. 68.

The late Ernst Buchner is responsible for the attribution of the present drawing to the Master of the Mühldorf Altar, an artist of the Danube area in the circle of Albrecht Altdorfer. The master is sometimes identified with Wilhelm Beinholt, whose death in 1521 is recorded on a gravestone in the Mühldorf parish church.[2] The technique and general character of this drawing are typical of the Altdorfer circle, and stylistically the drawing is very close to the Mühldorf Altar itself, which is dated 1511.[3]
Nothing is known of the earlier history of the drawing except that it was reproduced in an aquatint by Joseph Carl Burde in the nineteenth century.[4] Burde was patronized by the collector of drawings and prints, Count Sternberg of Prague, and it is likely that the study was at one time in the Count's collection. The drawing is laid down on the backs of four early engravings (now trimmed to the dimensions of the drawing, and therefore reduced to fragments). It is possible that the drawing was sold for the prints at one of the four sales of Sternberg's prints, held at Dresden between 1836 and 1842,[5] shortly before Edwin Crocker began buying drawings there.

[1] F.Brulliot, *Dictionnaire des monogrammes,* Munich, 1832-1834, no. 3176. [2] Neue Staatsgalerie, Munich, *Albrecht Altdorfer und sein Kreis,* 1938, 137. [3] Munich, *op.cit.,* cat. nos. 639-647 (illus.). See also the other works of the master reproduced, *ibid.,* cat. nos. 648-650, the *Sermon of Saint Paul,* Schweizerisches Landesmuseum, Zürich (illus., *Burlington Magazine,* 1921, XXXIX, 305, pl. B), and the altar in Santa Maria della Grazie, Germona (illus., H.Voss, "Uber den Ursprung der Bayerischen Renaissance Malerei," *Zeitschrift für bildende Kunst,* 1920, LV, 148 ff.). [4] Brulliot, *loc.cit.* [5] F.Lugt, *Repertoire des catalogues des ventes,* II, nos. 1435, 15177, 15802, 16714.   D.A.

25:101   KARL FRIEDRICH LUDWIG FELIX VON RUMOHR (1785–1843)   *Caricatures*

E. B. CROCKER ART GALLERY, SACRAMENTO. Museum No. 606-9.
241 x 191 mm.; pen and brown ink; inscribed on the verso by the artist, "Rosen auf den Weg gestreut/ und der Harm vergessen u. s. w./Gedenken Sie bei diesen Zeilen/ Ihres unvergesslichen Freundes/Carl Friedrich Schmahlgauer (?)/ zu Schweineburg".

The reputation of Baron Carl Friedrich von Rumohr rests primarily on his work as an art historian, art critic, translator of novels and collector of old master prints and

drawings. Throughout his lifetime, however, he also
produced drawings and etchings of animals, landscapes,
historical scenes and *Charakterköpfe*. The present drawing
falls into this last category. It is a small sheet of pen and ink
drawings on extremely thin letter paper containing forty-six
heads and four small half-length figures. The character
studies are all in frontal, three-quarter or profile view. Two
groups of heads (left center) form a caricature series in
which a single physiognomy is portrayed in six different
versions, each being a parody of the last. All kinds of
figures are represented, including some in military and
ecclesiastical dress; all kinds of attitudes are satirized —
boredom, disillusionment, anger, and cynicism; all ages
appear and all kinds of physiognomic types. The random
nature of the composition and the variety of finish and
subject matter suggest that the sheet was a storehouse of
impressions, perhaps intended for future use by the artist,
or perhaps as a simple display of virtuosity. The inscription
on the verso and the inappropriateness of the paper suggest
the latter may have been the case.   S.K.

26:103   JANUARIUS ZICK (1730–1797)   *Lazarus and the Rich Man,* ca. 1755–1760

E. B. CROCKER ART GALLERY, SACRAMENTO. Museum
No. 77-8.
180 x 292 mm.; pen and brown and grey ink and grey washes
heightened with white, on blue paper.
Exhibited: E. B. Crocker Art Gallery, Sacramento, *Old
Master Drawings from the E. B. Crocker Collection: The
German Masters, 15th to 19th Centuries,* 1939, cat. no. 64.

Traditionally called *The Return of the Prodigal Son,* the
subject of this scene is actually the parable of Lazarus and
the rich man (Luke 16:19-31). Lazarus is always shown
semi-recumbent in one corner of the composition, his sores
licked by dogs, as is the case here, and the rich man appears
feasting, often with his five brethren, on a raised loggia
above. Zick had done a somewhat different presentation
of the same scene in a drawing now in Düsseldorf,[1] in which
the brush washes are less restricted within the boundaries
of individual forms, the over-all tonality darker, and the
setting much more simplified. The moralizing thrust of the
story probably appealed greatly to Zick, who has been
characterized as a German Greuze.[2]
The function of the drawing is unknown. Feulner, in his
basic monograph on the Zick family, does not record any
painting of this subject.[3] The drawing must date from rather
early in the artist's career. The washes which model the
figures are not as loosely applied as in two drawings in
Coblenz from 1755.[4] On the other hand, the figure modeling,
especially that of Lazarus, already has something of the
knobby plasticity that later became characteristic of Zick.
He eventually became an early proponent of neo-classicism
in Germany and later eschewed such baroque forms as the
full, billowing curtain and the exuberant rococo ornament

in this drawing. Thus the drawing must date from soon after the studies in Coblenz. In fact, the ornament is similar to the stucco work at Amorbach where Zick and his father worked in the early fifties, and to a design by him for a wall decoration from about 1760.[5]

[1]Kunstakademie, Düsseldorf, *Beschreibender Katalog der Handzeichnungen,* 1930, cat. no. 1000. [2]O.Metzger, "Neue Forschungen zum Werk von Januarius Zick," *Wallraf-Richartz Jahrbuch,* 1966, XXVIII, 284. [3]A.Feulner, *Die Zick,* Munich, 1920. [4]Metzger, *op.cit.,* figs. 136, 137. [5]Feulner, *op.cit.,* respectively figs. 3, 12.   W.W.

27:104   GIOVANNI FRANCESCO BARBIERI, CALLED GUERCINO (1591–1666)   *David with the Head of Goliath,* ca. 1650

SANTA BARBARA MUSEUM OF ART. GIFT OF WRIGHT LUDINGTON. Museum No. 59.28.
306 x 422 mm.; red chalk; inscribed in a later hand, "Guercino" (bottom center).
Collections: Kleinberger Galleries, New York; Wright Ludington, Santa Barbara.

28:105   GIOVANNI FRANCESCO BARBIERI, CALLED GUERCINO   *King David,* ca. 1651

UNIVERSITY ART MUSEUM, UNIVERSITY OF CALIFORNIA, BERKELEY. Museum No. 1967.29.
241 x 292 mm.; corners missing and repaired; pen and brown ink.
Collections: Oswald Hughes-Jones, London; Charles E. Slatkin Galleries, New York.

Guercino produced many paintings and drawings of David, both as a young hero and as a King. There are Guercino drawings of David as the young hero, for instance, in the collections of the Louvre and the Fogg Art Museum,[1] as well as a painting of the same subject in a private collection at Guercino's birthplace, Cento.[2] However, there is no known Guercino representation of this subject that relates directly to the Santa Barbara drawing.
David as King is the subject of a Guercino drawing in the collection of the Earl of Leicester, and of a painting at Althrop in the collection of Earl Spencer.[3] The latter was commissioned from Guercino in 1651 by Giuseppe Locatelli of Cesena, and may well be the painting for which the Berkeley study was made.[4]

[1]Respectively: Louvre, no. 6862; A.Mongan and P.Sachs, *Drawings in the Fogg Art Museum,* Cambridge, 1940, I, 267.

[2]N.Grimaldi, *Il Guercino,* Bologna, n.d., pl. IX. There is record of a painting of this subject formerly in the collection of Lodovico Fermi, near Piacenza; C.C.Malvasia, *Felsina pittrice: vite de' pittori bolognesi,* Bologna, 1678, ed. here cited, Bologna, 1844, II, 269. [3]S.Bottari, R.Roli, and A.O.Cavina, *Guercino: Disegni,* Florence, 1966, pl. XI. The existence of the Althrop painting and its probable provenance were kindly brought to our attention by Mr. Denis Mahon. [4]Malvasia, *op.cit.,* II, 332.   J.St.

$29{:}106$ DOMENICO BECCAFUMI (1486–1551)   *Descent from the Cross,* ca. 1540

ACHENBACH FOUNDATION FOR GRAPHIC ARTS, CALIFORNIA
PALACE OF THE LEGION OF HONOR, SAN FRANCISCO.
367 x 279 mm.; torn in upper right corner; pen and brown
ink and wash, grey wash and black chalk; inscribed, "D.
Builfumi micarino cauato Del libro di vasari" (lower right).
Collections: Giorgio Vasari, Florence; Pierre Crozat, Paris;
Gabriel Huquier, Paris; James D. Phelan, San Francisco;
O'Hara-Livermore-and-Arthur, Inc., San Francisco.
Literature: H. Tietze, "A Drawing by Beccafumi in San
Francisco," *Pacific Art Review,* 1942, II, 7-9. *Exhibited:*
Mills College Art Gallery, Oakland, California, *Old Master
Drawings,* 1937, cat. no. 4; Portland Art Museum, Portland,
Oregon, *Old Master Drawings,* 1937, cat. no. 4; Pomona
College Art Gallery, Claremont, California, *Mannerism,*
1963; The John and Mable Ringling Museum of Art,
Sarasota, Florida, *Master Drawings,* 1967.

The inscription on the drawing refers to the collection of
Giorgio Vasari, who at the time of his death owned an
impressive collection of drawings bound in five folio
volumes. In his famous *Lives of the Artists* Vasari mentions
the collection several times and recalls among his drawings
some sheets by the hand of Beccafumi.[1] That a *Deposition*
was one of them is reported by Mariette in the auction
catalogue of the Crozat collection, which contained drawings
from both the Jabach and Vasari collections.[2] At the Crozat
sale in 1741 this particular drawing was purchased by the
art expert Huquier.[3] Its subsequent history until its
re-emergence in the possession of Senator Phelan is unknown.
Although there is no extant painting by Beccafumi of the
Descent from the Cross, the Achenbach drawing is not his
sole composition of the subject.[4] The National museum of
Stockholm owns a similar, somewhat smaller drawing which
bears an old attribution to Beccafumi.[5] A study of the upper
part of a *Deposition* by the master is preserved in the
Pinacoteca of Siena.[6] A third *Descent from the Cross* (The
Art Institute of Chicago) was attributed to the artist by
Horster, but is perhaps by another artist.[7]
Tietze refers to Marcantonio's engraving based on a
composition by Raphael (Bartsch, no. 32) as a source of
Beccafumi's composition. The Achenbach drawing certainly
shows Raphaelesque inspiration, but the influence of
Michelangelo is equally evident. Considering the Sienese

background of the master, however, it becomes clear that Sodoma's art more than any other served as Beccafumi's model. In fact, the mentioned drawing in Siena is a partial copy of Sodoma's *Descent* of 1513, painted for San Francesco in Siena and now in the Gallery there.[8] Beccafumi most probably also knew the *Deposition* by Rosso in Volterra.[9]

The value of the San Francisco drawing, however, does not lie in the mannerist blending of Raphael and Michelangelo, nor in the borrowings from other contemporary masters, but in the daring exploitation of the new pictorial possibilities of light and shade. Light is not created in the usual manner by heightening with white, but by flooding the pen drawing first with bistre and then with dark grey wash, allowing the uncovered paper to shine. The whole has the effect of a vision. The technique may be compared to the sheet representing the *Virgin and Child* in the Uffizi.[10] In both drawings agitated, supple lines are combined with energetic cross hatchings of straight long lines to indicate dark areas. The characteristic wash application with little regard for shapes and forms of figures can be found again in the studies for the pavements of Siena Cathedral.[11] Altogether the style is comparable to that of Beccafumi's late works, likewise built up from patches of light and shade.[12]

[1]Vasari, *Vite,* V, 653. [2]P.J.Mariette, *Description sommaire des dessins des grandes maîtres d'Italie, des Pays Bas et de France du Cabinet du feu M.Crozat,* Paris, 1741, 7. [3]A.Wyatt, "Le Libro de Disegni del Vasari," *Gazette des Beaux Arts,* 1859, IV, 350. [4]Tietze, *op.cit.,* 9. [5]O.Siren, *Italienska Handtekeningar,* Stockholm, 1917, cat. no. 228. [6]C.Brandi, "Disegni inediti di Domenico Beccafumi," *Bollettino d'Arte,* 1934, XXVII, 355, fig. 3. [7]M.Horster, "Eine unbekannte Handzeichnung aus dem Michelangelo Kreis und die Darstellung der Kreuzabnahme im Cinquecento," *Walraf-Richartz Jahrbuch,* 1965, XXVII, 225, fig. 162. [8]Illus., Venturi, *Storia,* IX, ii, 785, fig. 629. [9]Illus., Venturi, *op.cit.,* IX, v, 209, fig. 117. [10]Florence, Palazzo Strozzi, *Mostra Del Disegno Italiano di Cinque secoli,* 1961, cat. no. 53 (illus.). [11]R.de Liphart Ratshoff, "Un libro di schizzi di Domenico Beccafumi," *Rivista d'Arte,* 1935, XVII, 180, fig. 48; C.Brandi, *op.cit.,* 356, fig. 6. [12]Cf. Gibellino-Krascenimnicowa, *Il Beccafumi,* Florence, 1933, pls. 31, 32, 47.   E.G.

30:107   BERNARDO BELLOTTO (1720–1780)   *Capriccio of the Paduan Scene,* ca. 1740

COLLECTION MR. AND MRS. NORTON SIMON, LOS ANGELES.
191 x 324 mm.; reed pen and brown ink.
Collections: Mortimer Brandt Art Gallery.

The foreground of this drawing shows two low country houses on the left and an open embankment projecting into a river on the right. In the background, across the river, is a town. Along the edge of the embankment there are three buildings and a column with a statue.

The scene represents a "capricious" rearrangement of objects and landmarks appearing in an etching of Padua by Canaletto, Belotto's uncle.[1] The latter forms part of a series published between 1740 and 1743.[2] Belotto first worked with Canaletto in Padua around 1740,[3] and often copied or rearranged Canaletto compositions in his early work.[4] For example, there is an almost exact correspondence between Canaletto's drawing at Windsor Castle of Santa Giustina at Padua viewed from the ramparts,[5] and a drawing by Bellotto at Budapest.[6] The Budapest sheet is drawn with a very light line and has no hatching in the shaded areas, and is typical of Bellotto's drawing style as seen in his Dresden drawings and even in his drawing of *Vaprio e Canonico sull'Adda* in Warsaw.[7]

The Simon drawing, on the other hand, is done with muddy, heavy pen strokes, much closer to the style of Canaletto. The medium, however, is not handled with the transparency usually found in Canaletto's work. It is conceivable that at a very early period, around 1740, the young Bellotto might have been this strongly influenced by his uncle's style. The study is definitely from the circle of Canaletto and may represent one of the earliest known productions of Bellotto.

[1] R.Pallucchini and G.F.Guarnati, *Le Acqueforti del Canaletto,* Venice, 1945, pl. X. Cf. also, Fondazione Giorgio Cini, Venice, *Disegni Veneti del Settecento nella collezione Paul Walraf (Cataloghi di Mostre, 9),* 1959, cat. no. 16, and G.Spezzatti, *Le Ville Venete,* Venice, 1962, 308. [2] Pallucchini, *op.cit.,* 28. [3] H.A.Fritzsche, *Bernardo Bellotto detto il Canaletto* (dissertation, Martin Luther Universität), Halle/ Wittenberg, 1931, 25. [4] K.T.Parker, *The Drawings of Antonio Canaletto at Windsor Castle,* London, 1948, 44. [5] *Ibid.,* cat. no. 76. [6] Fondazione Giorgio Cini, Venice, *Disegni veneti del Museo di Budapest (Cataloghi di Mostre, 22),* 1965, cat. no. 99. [7] S.Kozakiewiez, "Catalogo dei disegni di Bernardo Bellotto," cat. nos. 1, 3, in, Palazzo Grassi, Venice, *Mostra di Bernardo Bellotto [e] Alessandro Gierymski,* 1955 (illus.). E.S.

31:108   REMIGIO CANTAGALLINA (CA. 1582–CA. 1635)   *Landscape with Seated Figures in Foreground*

THE LOS ANGELES COUNTY MUSEUM OF ART. Museum No. 60.13.
394 x 540 mm.; center fold, repaired; pen and brown ink; signed with the artist's monogram (lower left).[1]
Collections: Zeitlin & Ver Brugge, Inc., Los Angeles.

There are many known landscape drawings by Cantagallina, and they always employ the same repertoire of motives: large dark foreground trees (some gnarled and shattered), mound-like hillocks, and in the rear two or more vistas of light-bleached buildings and landscape forms. Cantagallina was active especially as an engraver, and produced a conspicuous body of landscape prints very much in the same style.[2] However, few of the known drawings relate to particular engravings, and many were presumably made for their own sake.

[1]Nagler, *Monogrammisten,* no. 3584. [2]Bartsch, *Peintre graveur,* XX, nos. 1-12.   D.T.

32:110
32v:111

VITTORE CARPACCIO (BEFORE 1472–BEFORE 1525)   recto: *Pope Alexander III Bestows a Ceremonial Parasol on Doge Sebastiano Ziani at Ancona,* 1507–1511
verso: the same

E. B. CROCKER ART GALLERY, SACRAMENTO. Museum No. 220-11.
210 x 294 mm.; trimmed on the left; pen and brown ink and wash (recto), pen and brown ink over red chalk (verso); inscribed, "Carpaccio" and "Perugino" (lower left, recto), "Verte" (lower right center, recto), "Vittore Carpaccio" (upper right, verso).
Collections: J. von Sandrart, Frankfurt and Nürnberg; I. G. Schuman, Dresden (Lugt 2344); Edwin Crocker, Sacramento.
Literature: E. Tietze-Conrat, "Decorative Paintings of the Venetian Renaissance," *Art Quarterly,* 1940, III, 20 (illus.); Tietzes, *Venetian Drawings,* no. 635 (illus.); E. Arslan, "Due disegni e un dipinto di Carpaccio," *Emporium,* 1952, CXVI, 109; G. Fiocco, *Carpaccio,* Novara, 1958, 35, no. 8; J. Lauts, *Carpaccio,* London, 1962, Drawings cat. no. 49 (illus.); M. Muraro, *Treasures of Venice,* Geneva, 1963, 140 (illus.); E. B. Crocker Art Gallery, Sacramento, *Catalogue of the Collections,* 1964, 54 (illus.).

The scene illustrated in this drawing is an episode from the war of 1176-1177 between Pope Alexander III and the Emperor Frederick III, called Barbarossa. In the mythology of the Venetian state this war came to be regarded as an epochal turning point in the rise of Venice to prominence as a world power. It was believed that Venice had obtained an end to the war and reconciled the two powers, although the facts of the story as set forth by Venetians were largely fanciful. During the sixteenth century, the entire history was depicted in a series of monumental canvases on the walls of the Hall of the Great Council in the Ducal Palace of Venice. Destroyed by fire in 1577, the series was replaced within a very few years by artists of the late sixteenth century.
The episode shown here follows the supposed reconciliation of Pope and Emperor at the entrance of the Basilica of San Marco, Venice. The peacemaking Doge, who accompanied the two sovereigns to Rome via Ancona, is being honored by the Pope with the gift of a parasol, an emblem of royal authority. In later times the parasol was an important part of the Venetian ducal regalia.
The Sacramento drawing studies the scene twice. On the recto the figures are large in proportion to the available field, the crowds of bystanders mass on the left and right, leaving the Pope and Doge, accompanied by the Emperor, isolated in the center. On the verso the figures are

proportionately smaller and the crowd closes behind and draws attention from the central group. It seems likely that the clearer and more monumental recto represents a later form of the design.

The recognition of this drawing and its purpose is due to Tietze-Conrat.[1] Both Gentile and Giovanni Bellini worked on the history cycle in the Hall of the Great Council and in 1507 Carpaccio is recorded as Giovanni's assistant in this Hall. In a letter of 1511 Carpaccio mentions the "Storia de Ancona" as a completed work of his own.[2] The two dates represent the outside dates of the painting and the Sacramento drawing.

Carpaccio's letter assures that the painting was his. There has been some controversy, however, over the authorship of the drawing. Gentile Bellini made sketches for some of the compositions in the Council room.[3] His figures are marked by cylindrical bodies and round heads. A drawing in this style, of a procession, in the Chatsworth Collection, has been attributed to Gentile by the Tietzes, Padre Resta, and von Hadeln, and to Carpaccio by Popham and Van Marle.[4] We can only say that Carpaccio's style is very similar to Gentile's in preliminary sketches. Since both Bellini brothers had been working on the compositions of the Sala before Carpaccio joined them, it is possible that one of them was responsible for the design of this composition. It may be that the verso, the more Bellinesque in style of the two sides of the drawing, is by Carpaccio after a first idea of Gentile. It has a broader conception of the whole composition with a processionary arrangement of the figures, as is common in the paintings of Gentile. The recto is more closely related to Carpaccio's undoubted drawings. Moreover, it is the source for another study, definitely by Carpaccio, of the two kneeling men on the right.[5]

[1]Tietze-Conrat, *loc.cit.* [2]G.Ludwig and P.Molmenti, *Vittorio Carpaccio,* London, 1907, 240. [3]Tietzes, *Drawings,* no. 263. [4]*Ibid.* [5]*Op.cit.,* no. 618.   E.S.

33:112
33v:113

ANNIBALE CARRACCI (1560–1609)   recto: *Study of a Hand Holding a Book,* after 1595
                                     verso: *An Elderly Man and a Hand*

Santa Barbara Museum of Art. Gift of Wright Ludington. Museum No. 65.34.
404 x 255 mm.; trimmed on the right; black chalk heightened with white chalk on faded blue paper.
Collections: Wawra auction, 1908; Archduke Friedrich von Hapsburg-Lothringen, Vienna; Adolph Loewi, Inc., Los Angeles.
Literature: J. Meder, *Handzeichnungen Alter Meister aus der Albertina und aus Privatbesitz,* N.F., I, Vienna, 1922, pl. 9; Palazzo dell'Archiginnasio, Bologna, *Mostra dei Carracci,* 1956, cat. no. 91.

This drawing has been claimed as the study for Annibale's small painting on copper. *The Vision of St. Francis,* in the collection of John Pope-Hennessy, London.[1] The painting can be dated shortly after Annibale's arrival in Rome in 1595, when he was in the service of Cardinal Odoardo Farnese. The study shows only the hand of the Virgin, holding a book with index finger pressed between the pages. The vigor with which the chalk is handled in boldly hatched strokes, and the coloristic use of the black shadows and white highlights to manipulate form, would relate this sheet in style to other drawings by Annibale of the late eighties and nineties. It is a style that differs noticeably from the softer, more grainy and painterly chiaroscuro character of earlier works, or the smoother, more controlled treatment with dark, fluid outlines found in so many of the later studies for the Farnese Gallery.

The studies on the verso of the Santa Barbara drawing do not seem to relate to any of Annibale's known works. A heavily robed, bearded, elderly man is shown rising from a seated position on the ground. His right hand reaches forward, while his head is inclined upward to his right. Above this figure another hand and wrist descend diagonally from the right corner.

[1]*Mostra dei Carracci, loc.cit.* Mr. Pope-Hennessy, in a letter to the compiler, has expressed doubt that the drawing is related to his painting or that it is by Annibale.   M.S.

34:114
34v:115   ANNIBALE CARRACCI   recto: *Landscape with Punting Boatman*, before 1595
                verso: *Mountain Landscape*

THE LOS ANGELES COUNTY MUSEUM OF ART. Museum No. 59.33.
250 x 413 mm.; pen and brown ink; inscribed, "Ticiano" (lower center left, verso).
Collections: Hanns Schaeffer Galleries, Los Angeles.
Literature: E. Feinblatt, "Recent Purchases of North Italian Drawings," The Los Angeles County Museum, Art Division, *Bulletin,* 1958, X, iii, 10-17.

As indicated by the old inscription on the verso, the drawing was once attributed to Titian, with whom this kind of landscape drawing is associated in sixteenth-century Italian art. The sheet can be dated fairly securely to Annibale's Bolognese period, just before the artist's departure for Rome in 1595, when his style came very close to that of his brother Agostino.[1] A very similar drawing of the period is the *Landscape with Jacob Asleep,* signed and dated 1595.[2] In both studies we find the same freely delineated cloud formations and horizontal hatchings between the clouds. The abbreviation—a curved cross—for flying birds is likewise common to both drawings. Compared with Agostino's drawings of the same period, such as the *Landscape with a Rocky Height,*[3] those by Annibale show less calculation and more sensitivity in the delineation of foliage and contours of mountains, with a correspondingly greater effect of spontaneity. Annibale's later Roman landscapes are more logically constructed and carefully drawn.

[1]Feinblatt, *op.cit.*, 12. [2]City of Leicester Museums and Art Gallery, *The Ellesmere Collection of Old Master Drawings*, 1954, cat. no. 64 (illus.). [3]*Ibid.*, cat. no. 39 (illus.). S.H.

35:109   JACOPO CHIMENTI, CALLED JACOPO DA EMPOLI (CA. 1554–1640)   *Queen Margherita of Spain arranging the Marriage of King Sigismund of Poland with her Sister, Constanza, 1612*

E. B. CROCKER ART GALLERY, SACRAMENTO. Museum
No. 219-29.
300 x 385 mm.; folded vertically and torn; black chalk, pen
and brown ink and wash, squared for transfer in red chalk.
Collections: Edwin Crocker, Sacramento.

Until now this drawing has been incorrectly attributed to
Federico Zuccari. It is the squared *modello* for a history
painting prepared in 1612, three years after Zuccari's death,
for the Florentine funeral rites of Queen Margherita of
Spain, wife of King Philipp III. Margherita was a sister of
Maria Maddalena of Austria, the wife of the Grand Duke
Cosimo II de' Medici of Florence. Her death therefore was
marked at Florence by an elaborate state funeral ceremony
in the Medici church of San Lorenzo, just as were the
deaths of princes of the late sixteenth and seventeenth
centuries who were linked to the Medici by political or
dynastic ties.
On this occasion the church was decorated with a series of
twenty-six grisailles illustrating events from the deceased
Queen's life, of which the scene represented in the present
drawing was the twenty-fourth. The entire set was
engraved and published at Florence in the same year,[1]
and the engraving of this particular scene was prepared by
Jacques Callot.[2]
The painting still survives in the magazines of the Palazzo
Pitti, Florence,[3] and is probably by Jacopo da Empoli,
who contributed to many of these state festival decorations.
Indeed, the drawing closely resembles his style. This may
be seen by comparing drawings for similar history paintings
executed by him on other occasions for the Medici. Thus,
the studies of the *Marriage of Catherine de' Medici* and the
Marriage of Marie de' Medici, both in the Uffizi, made in
1600 for paintings exhibited at Florence on the occasion
of the proxy-marriage of Marie, are drawn in the same
technique as the present drawing, similarly squared
for enlargement and identical in style.[4]

[1]G.Altoviti, *Essequie della sacra cattolica e real Maesta di Margherita d'Austria,* Florence (Sermartelli), 1612.
[2]*Op.cit.,* 35; cf. E.Méaume, *Recherches sur la vie et les ouvrages de Jacques Callot,* Paris, 1860, II, no. 452.
[3]Palazzo Pitti, no. 7804 (old no. 1327). [4]Uffizi, respectively, nos. 940 F, 941 F. For a full discussion of this cycle and illustrations, see A.F.Blunt, "A Series of Paintings . . . executed for Marie de Medicis," *Burlington Magazine,* 1967, CIX, 492-498, 562-566. The information in this catalogue entry is due entirely to the kindness of Miss Eve Borsook, who has generously shared with the compiler her

extraordinary knowledge of Medici festivals in the sixteenth and seventeenth centuries.

36:116
36v:117   PAOLO FARINATO (CA. 1524–AFTER 1606)   recto: *A Bishop Making an Offering of Bread and Wine*
   verso: *A Cleric Holding a Platter with a Calf*

E. B. CROCKER ART GALLERY, SACRAMENTO. Museum No. 280-24.
193 x 170 mm.; pen and brush and brown ink and wash heightened with white, on blue paper (recto); pen and brush and brown ink and wash (verso); inscribed in a modern hand, "Paul farinati" (lower left, recto), and "Ecole Venetienne" (middle, verso).
Collections: C. Gasc, Paris (Lugt 543); J. E. Gatteaux, Paris (Lugt 851); Edwin Crocker, Sacramento.

The bishop saint on the recto is complemented by the drawing on the verso which shows a bearded figure lying in a left-hand spandrel with a tiara beside him. The verso figure is looking to the left, but holds out to the right a platter with a calf upon it. Both figures (on recto and verso) presumably are intended for the same arch. Since both men look to the left, the probable placement of the arch would have been on the right wall of a church nave, where the figures would look toward the main altar.   E.S.

37:118   PIER LEONE GHEZZI (1674–1755)   *Caricature of a Gentleman*

THE LOS ANGELES COUNTY MUSEUM OF ART. Museum No. M.65.41.
324 x 229 mm.; pen and brown ink.
Collections: Adolph Loewi, Inc., Los Angeles.

Ghezzi may be considered the one Italian artist of his period who worked as a professional caricaturist. Unlike seventeenth-century artists such as Annibale Carracci, Guercino, and Bernini, who made caricatures on occasion, Ghezzi made a specialty of them and established a reputation in this genre.[1] He was the son of a painter (who had been president of the Accademia di San Luca) and was active as a painter, engraver, musician, antiquarian and decorator in the Vatican. His subjects belonged to the Rome of his day, including the Pope and his court, foreign visitors, artists and singers. There are thousands of Ghezzi drawings, the greatest number of which are in the Codice Ottobonioni of the Vatican Library. He also painted a series of frescoes in the Villa Falconieri at Frascati, in which caricature figures appear in a simulated architectural setting.[2] The subject of the present drawing has been called

Caricature of the French Ambassador to Venice, but the basis for the identification is unknown, and Ghezzi is not known ever to have been in Venice.[3] Most of the artist's good-humored satirizations are inscribed with pithy comments about the sitters, but there is no inscription here.

[1]A.F.Blunt and E.Croft-Murray, *Venetian Drawings of the XVII and XVIII Centuries . . . at Windsor Castle,* London, 1957, part II, "Venetian Caricatures," 139 ff. [2]M.Loret, "Pier Leone Ghezzi," *Capitolium,* 1935, XI, 291-307. [3]Blunt and Croft-Murray, *op.cit.,* 157.   M.S.

38:119   FRANCESCO GUARDI (1712–1793)   *Capriccio,* after 1780

THE LOS ANGELES COUNTY MUSEUM OF ART. Museum No. 57.46.
381 x 305 mm.; pen and brown ink and wash on dark grey paper.
Collections: Paul Kantor Gallery, Los Angeles.
Literature: E. Feinblatt, "A Romantic Capriccio by Guardi," The Los Angeles County Museum, Art Division, *Bulletin,* 1957, IX, iii, 3-5; The Los Angeles County Museum of Art, *Illustrated Handbook,* Los Angeles, 1965, 123-124.

The drawing is dominated by a large fountain partially in ruin which consists of a niche with columns on either side supporting an incomplete entablature. On the right, wide steps lead down into a shallow pond with ducks.[1] Behind a wall on the right are trees and a monument (like the column with Saint Theodore in the Piazzetta in Venice). To the left, behind the fountain, is a domed church.
Guardi made many such "capricious" drawings, composed of elements randomly selected from his repertoire of architectural and genre motives. The composition as a whole is similar to the title page from the etchings of Canaletto, *Vedute altre prese da i Luoghi altre ideate da Antonio Canal,* first published between 1740 and 1743.[2] Many of Guardi's ideas for the *capricci* are known to be derived from these etchings.[3] The difference in style between the two artists is very evident, however: Guardi is much more spontaneous, fanciful and free than Canaletto. The figures, drawn in very lively strokes, are similar to the many figures drawn by Guardi in the studies of the Museo Correr in Venice.[4] This loose style and lack of clear topographical reference are characteristic of Guardi's later period, around the 1780's.[5]

[1]E.Feinblatt, *op.cit.,* 5. [2]R.Pallucchini and G.F.Guarnati, *Le Acqueforti del Canaletto,* Venice, 1945, 28, pl. I. [3]J.Byam Shaw, *The Drawings of Francesco Guardi,* London, 1951, 30; Pallucchini and Guarnati, *op.cit.,* 26. [4]R.Pallucchini, *I disegni del Guardi al Museo Correr di Venezia,* Venice, 1943, e.g., no. 46. [5]J.Byam Shaw, *op.cit.,* 36.   E.S.

ACHENBACH FOUNDATION FOR GRAPHIC ARTS, CALIFORNIA
PALACE OF THE LEGION OF HONOR, SAN FRANCISCO.
GIFT OF E. B. MACDONALD.
347 x 478 mm.; numerous abrasions; pen and brown ink and
wash.
Collections: Galerie Cailleux, Paris; Frank Schwabacher,
Jr., San Francisco.

The drawing is related to a Guardi painting of the same
subject in the Louvre, which is in turn one of a series of
twelve paintings by him of Venetian ducal ceremonies and
festivals. The series derives from etchings made by Giovanni
Battista Brustoloni around 1763-1766 after drawings by
Canaletto.[1] The present sheet seems to be a copy of
the Louvre painting rather than a preparation for the
painting taken from Brustoloni's etching. The painting
copies the entire room as shown in the etching, while the
drawing reduces the size and depth of the room, omitting a
second large window and figure group on the left, a figure
on the right, and part of the ceiling. It is possible that
Guardi might have made a reduced drawing of one of his
paintings at the request of a buyer; it is unlikely, however,
that he would have copied the details of his own painting as
closely as this.[2] Even small distortions in the painting, like
that in the oval coffer in the ceiling decoration at the far end
of the room on the right, are faithfully reproduced. Each
figure in the drawing exactly matches the corresponding
figure in the painting, even in details like shadows on articles
of clothing. The rendering is more labored than in typical
Guardi drawings. The line itself, imitating Guardi's loose,
quick stroke, becomes exaggeratedly quivering, brittle,
and mannered.[3] It is possible that this copy of the painting
was made in Guardi's workshop, but no other example
of a similarly faithful copy from his studio is known. Also
the Louvre painting was copied in later times. A copy exists
in the collection of Charles de Marinitch, Paris, in which
the size and depth of the room are similarly reduced
as in this drawing.[4]

[1]W.G.Constable, *Canaletto,* Oxford, 1962, II, 328, explains
the relationship of the three artists, and mentions that
Canaletto's drawing of this particular number of the series
is one of two that are missing. Stylistically, there is of course
no possibility that this could be the missing Canaletto
drawing. V.Moschini, *Francesco Guardi,* Milan, 1952, pls. 77,
87, 88, reproduces the Brustoloni engraving and the Louvre
painting. [2]His only drawings relating directly to paintings
are quick studies that show his characteristic summary
indication of figures; cf. Moschini, pls. 162, 163, 164.
[3]Cf. J.Byam Shaw, *The Drawings of Francesco Guardi,*
London, 1951, e.g., pl. 39. [4]G.Fiocco, *Francesco Guardi,*
Florence, 1923, 54, pl. LII.   C.M.

The drawing is a study for a wall decoration that seems
intended to frame an illusionistic window or door. The
foreshortening indicates that the ensemble was meant to
stand on a large base above the ground, as in Lanfranco's
plan for the Benediction Loggia in Saint Peter's.[1] Several of
the hermae and human caryatids in the Benediction Loggia
support corbels with their arms crossed above their heads
and stand in similarly exaggerated *contrapposto* poses.
The architectural framework for the Benediction Loggia,
however, is more ornate than that of this drawing, and
satyrs are not included (and moreover would not have been
appropriate in an ecclesiastical commission). The particular
purpose for which this drawing was made is unknown.[2]
The summary treatment of the head and emphasis on the
torso of the satyr are characteristic of Lanfranco's drawings
of hermae and caryatids for wall decorations.[3] As usual,
he notes the basic composition for the drawing with a
nervous, rapid, red chalk underdrawing and then in pen
builds up the forms by reinforcing contours with quick
strokes which produce a characteristic staccato rhythm and
fragmented line.[4]

[1]For Lanfranco's complete plans for the Benediction Loggia
see, G.Lanfranco, *Disegno della loggia di San Pietro in
Vaticano, dove si da la benedizione . . . delineato et
intagliato da Pietro Santi Bartoli,* Rome, 1665. See further,
H.Hibbard, "The Date of Lanfranco's Fresco in the Villa
Borghese and other Chronological problems," *Miscellanea
Bibliothecae Hertzianae,* Vienna, 1960, 360, fig. 256 (illus.).
[2]A modern annotation on the verso of the Achenbach
drawing reads, "for the Farnese Gallery". Although
Lanfranco did begin his career as Annibale's assistant in
the Farnese Gallery, and often used hermae as they are
used there, there is no reason to assume that this caryatid
was drawn in connection with this work. The identification
may be owed to Hellman, *op.cit.,* since in his entry he refers
to a reproduction of a detail of the Farnese Gallery in
Charles Blanc's essay on Lanfranco. However, Blanc never
comments on his reproduction, which shows two male figures
supporting a ceiling and is in no way similar to this
drawing; cf. C.Blanc, *Histoire des peintres de toutes les
écoles,* XIII, *Ecole ombrienne et romaine,* Paris, 1884.
[3]E.g., W.Vitzthum, "A Project by Lanfranco for the
Quirinal," *Burlington Magazine,* 1964, CVI, 215 (illus.).
[4]J.Bean and W.Vitzthum, "Disegni del Lanfranco e del
Benaschi," *Bollettino d'Arte,* 1961, XLVI,
106-122 (illus.).   C.M.

ACHENBACH FOUNDATION FOR GRAPHIC ARTS, CALIFORNIA
PALACE OF THE LEGION OF HONOR, SAN FRANCISCO.
171 x 98 mm.; cut from a larger sheet, torn top edge, lower
right corner missing, laid down; pen and brown ink and
wash and white body color; inscribed in an old hand,
"Matturino" and "170" (verso).
Collections: Joseph Green Cogswell; Mortimer L. Schiff,
New York; Moore S. Achenbach, San Francisco.
Literature: Hellman, *Original Drawings,* cat. no. 96.

On the verso of this drawing there is an old attribution to
Maturino da Firenze who, with his more famous companion
Polidoro da Caravaggio, worked under Raphael during the
painting of the Vatican Loggia. The two artists were most
noted for the many Roman façade decorations they executed
together in the years immediately prior to the Sack of
Rome in 1527. The attribution of their drawings is made
especially difficult by the very nature of their commissions.
Since façade paintings are inherently perishable, little of
their work survives. Of some thirty façades they are known
to have painted, only one, that of the Palazzo Ricci,
survives in legible condition.[1] Often these paintings are
known only through accounts in the older sources,
particularly Vasari's life of Polidoro.[2] In other cases we
have their preparatory drawings or old engravings, although
it is frequently impossible to connect them with particular
projects. There are also a great number of copies by other
artists drawn either from the original sketches or from
the completed frescoes. The number of such copies, while
it demonstrates the high regard in which the artists were
held, complicates the problem of attribution, for all the
drawings have tended to be grouped around the more famous
name of Polidoro with the result that Maturino's
personality has been obscured.
The present drawing of an *Angel of the Annunciation* is a
case in point. It has been trimmed on all sides and must
originally have been completed by a figure of the Virgin
either to the left on the same sheet or, as is more likely
given the pose of the angel, on a separate sheet. The two
would then have been designed to form a related pair.
It is not possible to connect the drawing with any known
project. Perhaps it was a study for a façade; two separate
figures of the Virgin and Gabriel would conveniently fit the
spaces between a series of windows. One thing argues
against this suggestion, however. The majority of Maturino
and Polidoro's façade schemes were taken from Roman
history or mythology. Of the approximately thirty façades
which are known, the subjects of twenty have been
determined and only two were religious.[3] Equally, the
Annunciation is not a subject known to have been painted
by either Maturino or Polidoro in their few church
commissions.[4]
The drawing does clearly belong to the circle of Polidoro
and Maturino. Stylistically and technically it is close to
a drawing in Windsor Castle tentatively attributed to
Polidoro.[5] Thus there is no reason not to accept the
traditional attribution to Maturino. It could, in fact, be

the nucleus around which a corpus of Maturino drawings
might be assembled.

[1]Palazzo Braschi, Rome, Amici dei Musei di Roma, *Le case
romane can facciate griffite e dipinte,* 1960, is a catalogue of
all painted façades known to have existed in Rome.
[2]Vasari, *Vite,* V, 141-154. [3]*Le case romane, passim.* [4]Vasari,
op.cit., V, 147-148; C.Pacchiotti, "Nuove attribuzione a
Polidoro da Caravaggio in Rome," *L'Arte,* 1927, XXX, 189
ff., esp. 200 ff.; R.Kultzen, "Der Freskenzyklus in der
ehemaligen Kapelle der Schweizergarde in Rom," *Zeitschrift
für Schweizerische Archäologie und Kunstgeschichte,*
1961, XXI, 19 ff. [5]A.E.Popham and J.Wilde, *Italian
Drawings of the XV and XVI Centuries . . . at Windsor
Castle,* London, 1949, cat. no. 694, fig. 141.   K.T.

42:123   GIROLAMO FRANCESCO MARIA MAZZOLA, CALLED PARMIGIANINO (1503–1540)   *Seated Figure,*
before 1533

E. B. CROCKER ART GALLERY, SACRAMENTO. Museum
No. 232-11.
75 x 52 mm.; cut on all sides, torn, and laid down; pen and
brown ink and wash, yellow water color heightened with
white; illegible inscription (bottom center).
Collections: Edwin Crocker, Sacramento.
Literature: S. Freedberg, *Parmigianino,* Cambridge, Mass.,
1950, 196 (illus.).

Seated in a garland swing between two octagonal plaquettes,
this draped nude is one of several remaining preliminary
studies for the accessory figures on the soffits of the east and
west arches in the choir of Santa Maria della Steccata at
Parma. Parmigianino contracted to fresco the choir vault of
this church in 1531, and began the project with interest,
making a series of compositional drawings. In the end,
through his own dilatoriness and his disagreements with the
patrons, the project remained a fragment at his death
in 1540. This drawing, like the small drawings of accessory
figures in the Royal Library at Windsor,[1] was once part of a
larger sheet. It represents an intermediate stage in the design
of the accessory figures of the decoration.[2] The figure is
placed between octagonal plaquettes, as in an early design
for the vault at London, but it is no longer a *putto* as in the
London drawing.[3] On the other hand, the Sacramento
study must precede another drawing in London in which the
plaquettes are replaced by oval medallions.[4] Also the
Windsor studies for the accessory figures represent a later
phase, in that the figures stand erect rather than sit on the
edge of the plaquette, as they do in the first London drawing
and in the present sheet. In the second London drawing
they are likewise seen erect. All of these studies must date
between the time of the commission, 1531, and 1533, at
which time the form of the rosettes on the main part of the
vault had been finally determined in a different form
than they take in the studies we have cited.[5] The bold quick
strokes with brown ink and the sensitive, rhythmic modeling

with brown wash, white chalk and yellow water color are
typical of Parmigianino's drawings for the Steccata.

[1]A.E.Popham and J.Wilde, *The Italian Drawings of the XV and XVI Centuries . . . at Windsor Castle,* London, 1949, cat. nos. 588, 590 (illus.). [2]Cf. Freedberg, *loc.cit.* [3]British Museum, no. Ff-86; Department of Prints and Drawings, *Italian Drawings . . . : Artists Working in Parma in the Sixteenth Century,* London, 1967, cat. no. 126 (illus.): it can be dated before 1533. [4]British Museum, no. 1918-6-15-3; *op.cit.,* cat. no. 125. [5]Freedberg, *op.cit.,* 191; British Museum, *op.cit.,* cat. no. 126.   C.M.

43:124
43v:

JACOPO NEGRETTI, CALLED PALMA GIOVANE (1544–1628)   recto: *Three Figures in Ecstasy,* ca. 1580–1590

verso: *Figure Sketches*

E. B. CROCKER ART GALLERY, SACRAMENTO. Museum
No. 238-11.
92 x 86 mm.; cut at the top; pen and brown ink and wash
(recto), pen and brown ink (verso).
Collections: Edwin Crocker, Sacramento.
Literature: Tietzes, *Drawings,* no. 1138.

This drawing is typical of Palma's style and particularly
close to his drawings of the years 1580-1590. The rapid,
scribbled modeling pays little attention to extremities;
the heads and hands are hardly articulated. Beneath the
calligraphic flourishes, the pen stroke invariably remains
fragmented. As in his studies of these same years for
compositions of the *Brazen Serpent* and the *Massacre of the
Innocents,*[1] Palma models and enlivens the figures with
scratchy, zig-zag hatchings beneath a heavy wash, producing
a vibrant contrast with the white ground of the paper.
This strong chiaroscuro quality as well as the low vantage
point and diagonal structure of the composition reflect
Palma's interest in the art of Tintoretto in the 1580's and
1590's.[2] Neither the composition for which this study was
made, nor the subject it depicts, is known. The poses of
the three female figures, however, suggest a theme
of religious ecstasy.

[1]Tietzes, *op.cit.,* nos. 905, 829 (illus.); Galleria degli Uffizi, Gabinetto Disegni e Stampe, Florence, *Mostra di Disegni di Jacopo Palma Il Giovane,* 1958, fig. 19; Accademia Carrara, Bergamo, *Jacopo Palma Il Giovane Disegni Inediti,* 1964, pl. 110. [2]Tietzes, *op.cit.,* 191.   C.M.

COLLECTION R. L. BAUMFELD, LOS ANGELES.
245 x 173 mm.; upper right corner missing and repaired;
pen and brown ink; inscribed "La Pietà" (lower right).
Collections: L. Pollack, Rome (Lugt 788[b] on verso); Zeitlin
& Ver Brugge, Inc., Los Angeles.

The figure of Christ is shown in two positions: lying
diagonally on the ground, and in a half-seated position
supported by two or three figures. The theme of the
Lamentation was treated by Palma in numerous drawings
and paintings.[1] In particular, there is a more complete
drawing in the Louvre with a dead Christ seated, similarly
supported by three angels.[2] Another drawing much closer
in style to the present one is in the Leningrad Museum.[3]
The Leningrad sheet shows two sketches with angels
supporting Christ. His position and that of the angels varies
from sketch to sketch. Perhaps these two drawings, along
with the present sheet, represent various stages in the
development of a single composition. In that case, the
Baumfeld drawing would represent the first stage, because
it is the freest and least finished of the three.

[1]Cf. G.Guamlin, "Ritornando su Palma il Giovane," *Arte
Antica e Moderna,* 1961, XIII/XVI, 259-266; W.Heil,
"Palma Giovane als Zeichner," *Jahrbuch der Preuszischen
Kunstsammlungen,* 1926, XLVII, 58-71; Tietzes, *Drawings,*
nos. 871, 890, 897, 900, 956, 976, 1008, 1009, 1032,
1037-I-74, 1037-II-80, 250, 1040, 1092, 1093, 1094, 1165,
1168, 1169, 1205. [2]Musée du Louvre, Paris, *Le XVIe Siècle
européen: Dessins du Louvre,* 1965, cat. no. 116. [3]Fondazione
Giorgio Cini, Venice, *Disegni veneti del Museo di Leningrad
(Cataloghi di Mostre, 20),* cat. no. 28.   E.S.

45:126   GIULIO PIPPI, CALLED GIULIO ROMANO (1499-1546)   *A Sea Monster,* ca. 1524-1527

ACHENBACH FOUNDATION FOR GRAPHIC ARTS, CALIFORNIA
PALACE OF THE LEGION OF HONOR, SAN FRANCISCO.
165 x 171 mm.; cut from a larger sheet and at one time
folded in quarters; pen and brown ink with brown wash;
inscribed in various old hands, "Giovanni da Udine", "penna
di Andrea Mantegna", "80", and "291" (verso).
Collections: Joseph Green Cogswell; Mortimer L. Schiff,
New York; Moore S. Achenbach, San Francisco.
Literature: Hellman, *Original Drawings,* cat. no. 171.

This drawing was at one time attributed to Giovanni
da Udine, the sixteenth-century specialist in stucco work who
also did grotesques in the manner of antique decorations
in the ruins of the Palace of Nero on the Esquiline hill in
Rome. We might therefore expect to find such creatures in

his work. In fact, an engraving apparently after a drawing of a very similar though not identical monster, illustrates Charles Blanc's essay on Giovanni da Udine.[1] Unfortunately, it has proved impossible to trace the source of this illustration and to check the attribution. With this dubious exception, a similar creature does not occur elsewhere in Giovanni's oeuvre.

In the published catalogue of the Cogswell collection the drawing was again associated with Giovanni da Udine, and it was suggested that it may have been a study for a fountain for the Villa Madama, the Roman country house of Cardinal Giulio de Medici, where Giovanni is known to have executed two fountains.[2] However, the fountain in question is ornamented with a mosaic of sea shells and issues water from the trunk of an elephant, and does not seem to provide room for even a small sea monster, much less one as large as this, complete with reeds.[3]

In style and technique the sheet is much closer to the style of another Raphael pupil, Guilio Romano, who frequently used ink and wash binder, which Giovanni rarely did.[4] The handling agrees with that of a series of drawings for elaborate tableware executed by Giulio in Mantua between 1524 and 1526.[5] In these drawings there is not only a similar inventiveness in the creation of fantastic creatures, but also the same motive of the cattails (in a drawing for a bowl decorated with marine plants and foliage).[6] In addition, the sea monster is analogous to two dragon-like beasts occurring in Guilio's lunette fresco of 1527 of *Jove's Eagle Bringing to Psyche the Waters of the Styx,* in the Sala di Psyche of the Palazzo del Tè in Mantua.[7] The years 1524-1527 are a likely time for the present drawing as well.

[1]C.Blanc, *Histoire des peintres de toutes les écoles,* XIII, *Ecole ombrienne et romaine,* Paris, 1884, s.v. Giovanni da Udine, 1. [2]Hellman, *loc.cit.* [3]For a description of the fountain see, Vasari, *Vite,* VI, 556. [4]Typical drawings by Giovanni da Udine are illustrated in *The Vasari Society for the Reproduction of Drawings by Old and Modern Masters,* second series, 1929, X, pl. 5. [5]F.Hartt, *Giulio Romano,* New Haven, 1958, I, 87; II, figs. 130-145. [6]*Ibid.,* I, cat. nos. 92-93; II, figs. 142, 144. [7]*Ibid.,* I, 87; II, fig. 251 (illus.). Cf. also the studies, I, cat. nos. 168-169; II, figs. 271-272.   K.T.

46:128   FRANCESCO DA PONTE, CALLED BASSANO (CA. 1549–1592)   *Woman on Horseback*

E. B. CROCKER ART GALLERY, SACRAMENTO. Museum No. 233-28.
360 x 265 mm.; black chalk and brown wash on blue paper heightened with white; inscribed in an eighteenth-century hand. "J. Bassano" (lower left).
Collections: A. J. Dézallier Dargenville, Paris; Destouches, Paris; Edwin Crocker, Sacramento.
Literature: A. Neumeyer, "A Bassano Drawing," *Old Master Drawings,* 1939, XIII, 61; Tietzes, *Drawings,* no. 195;

W. Arslan, *I Bassano,* Milan, 1960, I, 176. *Exhibited:* The
Art Gallery of Toronto, *Sixteenth Century Venetian
Drawings,* 1960; Seiferheld Gallery, New York, *An
Exhibition of Bassano Drawings,* 1961, cat. no. 4.

The present drawing is related to a figure that appears in
several paintings by members of the prolific Bassano family.
The cooperative and imitative work patterns in the family
workshop have caused considerable confusion in the study of
the workshop output, and this drawing exemplifies the
problem.

Alfred Neumeyer believed the study to be a preliminary
drawing by Jacopo (the chief artist of the family) for the
Dresden painting, *The Israelites in the Desert,*[1] which
shows a woman in the same position but with a child behind
her on the horse. The Tietzes, on the other hand, relate
the drawing to another painting of the same subject ascribed
to Jacopo's son, Francesco Bassano, in the Kunsthistorisches
Museum in Vienna.[2] As Rearick has pointed out, however,[3]
the drawing corresponds precisely to neither of these
paintings, but rather to a figure in Francesco's picture of the
Departure for Canaan, in the Rijksmuseum, Amsterdam.[4]
Hence it must be a copy after that painting, and presumably
was made to serve as a *ricordo,* or record, of a motive that
might be re-used in later works. The figure was indeed
re-used by Francesco in the painting at Vienna
mentioned above.

The motive was not invented by Francesco. It was taken
over by him from the *Departure for Canaan* in West Berlin,
a picture signed jointly by father and son, Jacopo and
Francesco, but invented by the former and thus the
archetype of the series.[5]

[1]Neumeyer, *op.cit.,* Arslan, *op.cit.,* II, pl. 210. [2]Arslan,
op.cit., II, pl. 285. [3]Professor Rearick generously shared
with the compiler all his knowledge of the Bassano shop as
it bears on the present drawing, by replying to our written
inquiry. [4]No. 434-D-1; Arslan, *op.cit.,* II, pl. 270.
[5]No. 4/60.   J.St.

47:127   GIUSEPPE DELLA PORTA, CALLED SALVIATI (CA. 1520–CA. 1575)   *Figures before an Altar*

E. B. CROCKER ART GALLERY, SACRAMENTO. Museum
No. 278-12.
286 x 216 mm.; laid down; pen and brown ink and wash
heightened with white, on blue paper, squared in red chalk.
Collections: Nicolas Lanier, London (Lugt 2886); Edwin
Crocker, Sacramento.
Literature: Tietzes, *Drawings,* no. 1392; E. B. Crocker Art
Gallery, Sacramento, *Italian Masters,* 1959; M. H. de Young
Memorial Museum, San Francisco, *Man: Glory, Jest and
Riddle,* 1965, cat. no. 94.

The subject of the drawing is uncertain. The Tietzes entitle
it "subject unknown." Bohr considered it a scene of

"figures before a well."[1] However, the attitudes of the figures and the shape of the block on the right make it more likely that an altar is intended, and that the drawing represents an offering or sacrifice.

The sun reveals and a key unlocks, and in this sense these are traditional symbols of, respectively, the concept of Truth and the ancient god Janus, the guardian of all doorways and paths.[2] A vase, when letting forth flames, is a symbol of the love of God.[3] In the present drawing the sundisc stands in relation to the three vases as would smoke or fire issuing from them. Thus, a likely interpretation of the scene is as an allegory of the love of God as a path to truth, opened to a searching humanity (the figures on the left) by a priesthood (the officiating figure). If this interpretation is correct, it is significant for the epoch of the drawing that the notions of sacrifice, truth and God are expressed entirely in neutral, non-Christian terms.

The red chalk squaring indicates that the drawing was a finished composition, ready for transfer to a larger surface. Salviati was employed at Venice especially as a painter of house façades, and the character of the composition is not unlike some of his other decorations on the fronts of buildings. The drawing may tentatively be related to a series of destroyed frescoes on a house near, and belonging to, the Scuola di San Rocco at Venice, for which Salviati received two payments in 1551.[4] This house was described by Ridolfi, in his lives of the Venetian artists of 1648, as having "a sacrifice of the Sun and of Cain" painted on its façade.[5] However, a single scene with a sacrifice of the Sun and Cain makes no sense. Boschini's guide book to Venice for 1674 describes the same house and mentions two paintings of the Old Testament, of which one was a sacrifice of Cain.[6] Thus, it is possible that Ridolfi combined two separate scenes, a sacrifice of Cain and another in which a sacrifice of the sun was depicted, for which this drawing may be the preliminary study.

[1]Tietzes, loc.cit.; R.L.Bohr, *The Italian Drawings of the E.B.Crocker Art Gallery Collection, Sacramento, California,* unpublished Ph.D. dissertation, University of California, Berkeley, 1958, 204, no. 153. [2]G.de Tervarent, *Attributs et symboles dans l'art profane,* Geneva, 1958-1959, respectively, II, col. 356, and I, col. 100. [3]*Ibid.,* cols. 396-398. [4]G.Nicoletti, *Illustrazione della Chiesa e Scuola di San Rocco in Venezia,* Venice, 1885, 61-62. [5]C.Ridolfi, *Le Maraviglie dell'Arte,* Venice, 1648, ed. here cited, ed. D.von Hadeln, Berlin, 1914-1924, I, 241. [6]M.Boschini, *Le Ricche Minere della Pittura Veneziana,* Venice, 1674, San Polo, 54.   K.T.

48:129   MATTIA PRETI (1613–1699)   *Head of an Old Man,* ca. 1650–1651

LOEWI-ROBERTSON, INC., LOS ANGELES.
191 x 140 mm.; red chalk (counterproof).
Collections: Unidentified (Lugt 609); R. Lamponi, Florence,

and E. R. Lamponi-Leopardi, Turin (Lugt 1760); A. Klein, Frankfurt (Lugt 2786b).

The particular charm of this unassuming little sketch is in the smooth velvety handling of the shading and the sensitive tonal modeling of the face which produce an almost painterly quality without really being painterly in style. At the same time a freer, more open, almost scribbly type of chalk stroke, characteristic of a simplified and abstract quality in many of Preti's drawings, is used here in hair and beard. As a counterproof, i.e., a reverse copy taken from an original chalk drawing by a wet press method, the image on this sheet is no doubt softer and more fragile in appearance than the original drawing, and certainly the graphic line and the tonal contrasts are less assertive and less strong than in most of the artist's known drawings.

The drawing style somewhat resembles that of the *Resurrected Christ* in the Albertina,[1] or of the *Figure of a High Priest with Studies of Two Heads* in the Louvre.[2] The idealization of the face, however, places this drawing in an earlier period of Preti's complex development, prior to his trip to Naples in 1656. It probably dates from the early fifties, either when he was still in Rome working on his wall frescoes for Sant' Andrea della Valle (1650-1651),[3] or in Modena working on the cupola decorations for San Biagio.[4] By then Preti had outgrown his Caravaggesque characteristics of the 1630's. In addition to the neo-Venetian influences to which he had then been introduced, he was still much under the influence of an early trip to Emilia, and the work of Bolognese artists at Rome, evidence of which is clear in this drawing.

The specific subject for this head is not known, nor is there any indication whether the original drawing, from which this sheet derives, still survives. The study has been ascribed to José de Ribera ("Lo Spagnoletto," 1591-1652), but there is no convincing reason for such an attribution.

[1] A.Spitzmüller and A.Stix, *Beschreibender Katalog der Handzeichnungen in der Staatlichen Graphischen Sammlung Albertina,* vol. VI, *Die Schulen von Ferrara, Bologna, Parma und Modena, der Lombardei, Genuas, Neapels und Siziliens,* Vienna, 1941, fig. 584. [2] N.Ivanoff, *I disegni italiani del Seicento, scuole veneta, lombarda, ligure, napoletana,* Venice, 1959, pl. 99. [3] *The Crucifixion of Saint Andrew;* illus., R.Longhi, *Scritti giovanili,* Florence, 1962, II, pl. 15. [4] Musée du Louvre, Paris, Cabinet de Dessins, *Le dessin à Naples du XVIe siècle au XVIIIe siècle,* 1967, pl. XV; R.Causa, "Per Mattia Preti: il tempo di Modena ed il soggiorno a Napoli," *Emporium,* 1952, CXVI, 201-212, figs. 1-4.   M.S.

49:130   GUIDO RENI (1575–1642)   *Dido and Aeneas,* ca. 1621

ACHENBACH FOUNDATION FOR GRAPHIC ARTS, CALIFORNIA PALACE OF THE LEGION OF HONOR, SAN FRANCISCO. 318 x 380 mm.; trimmed on all sides, folded vertically, and

torn; black chalk; inscribed by a later hand below the figures, "didone" and "enea" (recto), and "53" (verso).
Collections: Joseph Green Cogswell (mark on verso); Mortimer L. Schiff, New York; Moore S. Achenbach, San Francisco.
Literature: Hellman, *Original Drawings,* cat. no. 126.

The subject is based on Virgil's *Aeneid,* and shows the Carthaginian queen Dido attempting to dissuade her lover Aeneas from leaving her and so fulfilling his destiny. The drawing is attributed to Reni, and exhibits some of that same enthusiasm for the secular themes of antiquity and is rendered with that same lively style found in his paintings of the early 1620's (particularly in his *Nessus and Dejanira* in the Louvre, painted in 1621 for the Duke of Mantua). Light is rendered with great sensitivity, movement is graceful, and the figures are lithe. The drawing is handled with a delicacy of touch surpassing even that found in the paintings. None of Reni's known works corresponds directly to this drawing, but there is an attributed painting of this period, the *Meeting of Dido and Aeneas* in Kassel, Staatliche Kunstsammlungen, which bears some resemblance in facial type, though not as much in style or dress.[1] Malvasia mentions among other *bozze* by Reni one showing the *Flight of Aeneas,* belonging to Alessandro Fava.[2] Whether the artist worked on other scenes dealing with Aeneas is not known, but the inspiration for such might have come from the Carracci frescoes in the Palazzo Fava, in which subjects from the Aeneid were depicted.
Drawings by Reni are surprisingly scarce and mostly functional studies, indicating a lack of interest in drawing per se.[3] The purpose of this rather unusual but lovely drawing hence is problematical.

[1]Palazzo dell'Archiginnasio, Bologna, *Mostra di Guido Reni,* 1954, cat. no. 22. [2]C.C.Malvasia, *La Felsina Pittrice: vite de' pittori bolognesi,* Bologna, 1678; ed. here cited, Bologna, 1844, I, 63. [3]R.Causa, "Unpublished Drawings by Guido Reni," *Art Quarterly,* 1955, XVIII, 53-61.   M.S.

50:131
50v:
SEBASTIANO RICCI (1659–1734)   recto: *A Saint Transported on a Cloud*
                                 verso: *Nude Male Figure with Outstretched Arms*

UNIVERSITY ART MUSEUM, UNIVERSITY OF CALIFORNIA, BERKELEY. Museum No. 1967.42.
273 x 208 mm.; cut on the bottom and right; red chalk, pen and brown ink and wash (recto), red chalk (verso); inscribed with a mathematical calculation (recto), and "N 9" "1967.42" (lower right, verso).
Collections: Zeitlin & Ver Brugge, Inc., Los Angeles.
Literature: "College Museum Notes, Acquisitions, Drawings," *Art Journal,* 1967/1968, XXVII, 202.

Clearly a sketch for a ceiling painting, the drawing represents the apotheosis of a bearded saint. Two putti hover below and a putto on the left carries a papal tiara and another on the right a palm of martyrdom. Ricci's only known ceiling painting of an apothesis is the central canvas in the nave of the church of San Marziale in Venice of ca. 1703-1705.[1] The drawing cannot be a preliminary study for this composition, however, as Saint Martial was a bishop, while the tiara in the present study is the attribute of a pope. The style of the drawing, moreover, is that of Ricci's later years when he frequently used the medium of red chalk overlaid with pen and ink and wash.[2] While the line is perhaps not as cursive or agitated as it is in most of his late drawings, it does seem comparable to the studies for a *Ressurrection* or for the *Aurora,* both at Windsor Castle.[3] They are executed in pen and ink and wash over black chalk, and are datable to ca. 1710 and ca. 1720 respectively.[4] The study on the verso of a nude man with arms outstretched standing on a bank of clouds and enclosed by a tentatively-drawn frame, seems the first in sequence of time. Ricci next turned the sheet over and in the lower right corner, now partially cut away, redrew the figure of the saint in pen and ink, changing the pose to a seated one and adding the drapery. He then drew the final and most detailed study, which the pen sketch forced him to offset toward the left edge of the sheet, laying out the drawing in red chalk and then working over these guide lines with pen and ink and wash. In the chalk underdrawing slight but significant alterations are introduced in the axis of the torso, movement of the knees, head and arms. There are also changes introduced between the chalk underdrawing and the ink overlay. The most important was the elimination of the single putto sketched in the lower lobe of the frame. This removes a drag on the upward movement of the composition, and gives greater concentration to the main group.

[1]J.von Derschau, *Sebastiano Ricci ein Beitrag zu den Anfängen der venezianischen Rokokomalerei,* Heidelberg, 1922, 68, fig. 34; R.Pallucchini, *La Pittura Veneziana del Settecento,* Venice and Rome, 1960, 12, fig. 8. Derschau dates the painting to between the end of the 1690's and 1705; Pallucchini places it ca. 1703-1704 and definitely before 1705. [2]A.F.Blunt and E.Croft-Murray, *Venetian Drawings of the XVII and XVIII Centuries . . . at Windsor Castle,* London, 1957, 47. [3]*Ibid.,* cat. nos. 342, 274 (illus.). [4]For Ricci's late drawing style generally see, *ibid.,* 47.   K.T.

51:132   ANDREA SCHIAVONE (CA. 1505–1563)   *Standing Prophet in a Niche*

E. B. CROCKER ART GALLERY, SACRAMENTO. Museum No. 277-29.
357 x 170 mm.; laid down; black chalk heightened with white, on blue paper, squared for transfer in black chalk.
Collections: Edwin Crocker, Sacramento.

The drawing represents a bearded prophet figure, turned three-quarters to the right, standing in a niche and holding in his hands a long scroll. In a manuscript catalogue of the

Crocker collection, it is listed as an anonymous sixteenth-century central Italian drawing. An old attribution on the mount ascribes it to Salviati, by which the Venetian Salviati, whose real name was Giuseppe della Porta (no. 47 in the present catalogue) was presumably meant.[1] In style, however, it seems to be much closer to Andrea Schiavone, whose art reflects the influence of Parmigianino and the north Italian mannerists.

Although the use of chalk necessarily produces a softer effect than Schiavone's favorite medium of ink and brush with white body color, the elongation of the figure and the painterly modeling are typical of his drawing style.[2] If one makes allowance for the difference in medium, this drawing seems particularly close to an ink and wash drawing of a draped female figure in the Budapest Museum of Fine Arts.[3] The non-structural nature of the figure is paralleled in Schiavone's prints, for example, the set of *Christ and the Apostles* (Bartsch 38-50).[4]

The drawing is squared, indicating that it was a final design ready for enlargement. It may well have been intended as a study for one of the fourteen paintings of prophets in niches which ornament the walls of the reading room of the Libreria di San Marco in Venice. This series was probably begun ca. 1560 and includes two figures by Schiavone and others by Veronese, Tintoretto and other unidentified artists.[5] Although the drawing does not agree with either of the surviving Schiavone paintings, it could be a rejected version or perhaps the study for a third prophet by Schiavone which, according to Boschini, was destroyed and later replaced by another by Pietro della Vecchia.[6]

[1]R.L.Bohr, *The Italian Drawings in the E.B.Crocker Art Gallery Collection, Sacramento, California,* unpublished Ph.D. dissertation, University of California, Berkeley, 1958, 240. [2]For a corpus of photographs of Schiavone drawings see L.Frölich-Bum, "Andrea Meldola gennant Schiavone," *Jahrbuch der Kunsthistorischen Sammlungen des Aller-höchsten-Kaiserhauses,* 1913, XXXI, 137 ff. [3]Cf. I.Fenyo, *North Italian Drawings from the Collection of the Budapest Museum of Fine Arts,* Budapest, 1965, 73, pl. 35. [4]Bartsch, *Peintre graveur,* XVI, nos. 38-50. [5]D.von Hadeln, "Beiträge zur Tintorettoforschung," *Jahrbuch der Königlich Preuszischen Kunstsammlungen,* 1911, XXXII, 32, 37; see figs. 2-3 for Schiavone prophets. [6]Von Hadeln, *op.cit.,* 29; G.Lorenzetti, *Venezia ed il Suo Estuario,* Rome, 2, 1956, 152, suggests the destroyed canvas was probably by Tintoretto.   K.T.

52:133   LUCA SIGNORELLI (CA. 1450-1523)   *Seated Female Figure,* ca. 1499

COLLECTION NORTON SIMON FOUNDATION, FULLERTON. 220 x 170 mm.; top left and top right corners torn, cut on left and right; black chalk on pale blue paper. *Collections:* W. H. Schab Gallery, New York.

Although the figure in this drawing cannot be linked directly with a figure in a painting by Signorelli, the position of the seated figure recalls the poses of certain saints in the vault frescoes of the Cappella di San Brizio, Orvieto Cathedral, where Signorelli began work in 1499.[1] The sureness and solidity of figure drawing is characteristic of the artist. One might compare the present figure with his drawing of a *Madonna and Child with the Little Saint John* in the Uffizi.[2] However, it lacks the hard-edged line which is characteristic of many of Signorelli's later drawings for the Orvieto frescoes. Here the edges are softer and more blurred, creating a more sensuous effect.[3] (The attribution of the drawing is due to Otto Benesch and Paul Sachs.)[4]

[1]Cf. M.Salmi, *Luca Signorelli,* Novara, 1953, pls. 39-40. [2]*Mostra di Luca Signorelli,* Cortona, 1953, 144. [3]Cf. the black chalk drawing of *Apollo,* Uffizi, no. 130 F. (illus., *ibid.,* 132). [4]Written opinion in the files of the Norton Simon Foundation.   L.O.

53:134
53v:135   PELLEGRINO TIBALDI (1527–1596)   recto: *Female Figure with Flying Drapery and Raised Arms*

verso: *Female Figure with Flying Drapery and Raised Arms, a Male Head, and Figure Sketches*

THE LOS ANGELES COUNTY MUSEUM OF ART. Museum No. 60.74.
330 x 279 mm.; top corners torn and repaired, cut on the bottom and right; pen and brown ink and wash; inscribed in several old hands, "+ di Batsasar da Siena" (top left, recto), "12" (lower left, recto), "158" (center bottom, recto), "68" (lower right, recto), "217" (top right, verso), "Rafaello de Reggio" (center right, verso), "6 R" (center bottom, verso), and "1232" (lower left, verso).
Collections: Count R. de Villette, Paris (Lugt 2200ᵃ); Hanns Schaeffer Galleries, Los Angeles.
Literature: E. Feinblatt, "A Drawing by Pellegrino Tibaldi," The Los Angeles County Museum, Art Division, *Bulletin,* 1961, XIII, ii, 3-12; W. Ames, *Drawings of the Masters: Italian Drawings from the 15th to the 19th Century,* New York, 1963, 110; The Los Angeles County Museum of Art, *Illustrated Handbook,* 1965, 122.

The two main figures on the recto and verso of this drawing are preliminary sketches for one of the four flower-bearing figures appearing in Tibaldi's vault fresco of the early 1550's in the Sala delle Adunanze of the Palazzo Poggi, Bologna.[1] The figure on the verso is closer to the finished work, although elements from the study on the recto survive into the fresco as well. Pellegrino's "touch" contributes to the dynamism of the figures. Light washes are floated around the legs of the figure on the recto and then are overlaid with darker pen strokes and supplementary washes which define the major shadows. Often, as in the head, hair and folds of the garment, the irregular patches of wash suggest form more powerfully than the few pen lines.
The drawing in the lower right-hand corner of the verso lacks washes, but uses the same scratchy line as the principal

study. Ebria Feinblatt considers the pen sketch earlier than the large figure, because the latter is displaced to the left side by the group.[2] The observation is well taken, though it would seem that both drawings are roughly contemporary. A preliminary pen study for *The Sermon of Saint John the Baptist,* painted about the same time as the Palazzo Poggi vault,[3] is entirely similar in style, There too, tangled groups of figures are indicated by a loose web of lines, and contours become a snarl of long straggly strokes.

The head in the lower left-hand corner of the verso is vaguely reminiscent of the bearded male heads with prominent moustaches that appear in the Palazzo Poggi frescoes of *The Shipwreck of Ulysses* and *Aeolus and Ulysses.*[4]

[1]The identification is owed to H.Voss; cf. Feinblatt, *loc.cit.* For the frescoes, see G.Briganti, *Il mannerismo e Pellegrino Tibaldi,* Rome, 1945, 77 ff., fig. 123. [2]Feinblatt, *loc.cit.* [3]The Metropolitan Museum of Art, New York, and The Pierpont Morgan Library, New York, *Drawings from New York Collections,* I, *The Italian Renaissance,* 1965, cat. no. 122 (illus.). [4]Illus., Briganti, *op.cit.,* figs. 115, 117.   D.T.

54:136   GIOVANNI BATTISTA TIEPOLO (1696–1770)   *Adoration of the Magi*

STANFORD UNIVERSITY MUSEUM. MORTIMER C. LEVENTRITT COLLECTION.
290 x 205 mm.; pen and brown ink and wash over pencil.
Collections: Mortimer C. Leventritt, San Francisco.

Undoubtedly one of the leading painters and the most famous and skillful decorator of eighteenth-century Europe, Giambattista Tiepolo was a prolific draughtsman as well. His development in the medium paralleled his development as a painter. The early drawings, like the Stanford *Adoration of the Magi,* show a synthesis of elements taken from his great Venetian predecessors, but with hesitant handling and frequent reworkings.

The compositional format of the present drawing is a free translation of Sebastiano Ricci's *Adoration* at Hampton Court, not only in the disposition of the figures, but also in such details as the cherubim and light rays in the sky, the turban on the ground at the lower left, and the presence of camels and halberds at the right. All these motives ultimately go back to the repertoire of Paolo Veronese. The latter is a direct source for the kneeling Magus in the foreground and the turbaned figure leaning forward, both of which are derived from an *Adoration* by Veronese in the Kunsthistorisches Museum at Vienna.

The repetition of lines in this drawing creates a less powerful effect than is customary in the work of Tiepolo. He changed the leg of the Moorish servant at the right several times to achieve a more dramatic pose. The uncertain lines and uneconomical use of washes suggest a very early date for the Stanford drawing, some years earlier still than a drawing of the same subject in The Metropolitan Museum of Art, dated to the 1730's by Benesch.[1] No youthful paintings of the *Adoration* are known, although Tiepolo returned to the subject later in his career.

[1]O.Benesch, *Venetian Drawings of the Eighteenth Century in America,* New York, 1947, 30. Also T.Pignatti has expressed the opinion that the Stanford drawing is an early work. N.R.

55:137 GIOVANNI BATTISTA TIEPOLO *Adoration of the Magi,* 1753

ACHENBACH FOUNDATION FOR GRAPHIC ARTS, CALIFORNIA PALACE OF THE LEGION OF HONOR, SAN FRANCISCO.
404 x 293 mm.; laid down; black chalk and pen and brown ink and wash; inscribed in a modern hand, "Tiepolo, Giovanni Battista, L'Adoration des Mages" (verso).
Collections: Mrs. Charles T. Crocker, San Francisco.

When the Benedictine Church of Schwarzach commissioned from Tiepolo an *Adoration of the Magi* in 1753, the artist seems to have become fascinated with the possibilities of this particular subject. He produced several drawings and two paintings of the *Adoration,* and Pignatti has recently added the large etching of an *Adoration* to this period for stylistic reasons.[1] The San Francisco drawing is most closely related to the etching, and is either a preparatory sketch for it or derives from it.
The pose of the turbaned figure bowing in reverence is identical in both the drawing and the etching; the Madonna and servant boy are changed only very slightly; columns and wooden beams form the backdrop of both settings; and the unusually large size of the drawing is close to that of the etching (412 x 283 mm.). But there are certainly notable differences. In the drawing Tiepolo used a similar composition, larger in scale though more intimate in spirit, and employed washes fluently to define the contours of the figures and to create a rich coloristic effect, while in the etching he chose to emphasize texture with the use of short choppy strokes.
Sebastiano Ricci's *Adoration* at London again served as a point of departure for Tiepolo. He incorporated its basic format and borrowed many details, but drastically reduced the number of participants and varied their poses.

[1]The painting now in the Alte Pinakothek, Munich; cf. A.Morassi, *A Complete Catalogue of the Paintings of Giovanni Battista Tiepolo,* London, 1962, 30. For the etching, see T.Pignatti, *Le Aquaforti dei Tiepolo,* Florence, 1965, pl. 1, with commentary. N.R.

GIOVANNI BATTISTA TIEPOLO   recto: *The Crucifixion*, ca. 1745–1750

verso: *Torso for the Figure of the Crucified Christ*

ACHENBACH FOUNDATION FOR GRAPHIC ARTS, CALIFORNIA
PALACE OF THE LEGION OF HONOR, SAN FRANCISCO.
364 x 254 mm.; trimmed on all four sides; pen and brown
ink and wash over pencil (recto), pen and brown ink
(verso).
Collections: Prince Orloff, Leningrad; Marquis de Biron;
W. W. Crocker, San Francisco.
Literature: D. von Hadeln, *Handzeichnungen von Giovanni
Battista Tiepolo,* Munich, 1927, no. 96 (illus.); G. Knox,
"The Orloff Album of Tiepolo Drawings," *Burlington
Magazine,* 1961, CIII, 273.

The drawing is very close to the *Crucifixion* in the City Art
Museum of St. Louis, while the motive of the bad thief
reappears in the *Crucifixion* in the van Beuningen
Collection.[1] Both paintings date from the years 1745-1750.
The heavy forms and the dissolution of the line with wash
are characteristic of this period. They may be found again
in the drawings just preceding Tiepolo's work in Würzburg,
for example, the drawing of a group of standing figures
in the Victoria and Albert Museum, London.[2]

[1] A.Morassi, *A Complete Catalogue of the Paintings of
Giovanni Battista Tiepolo,* London, 1962, respectively, 47, 66.
[2] G.Knox, *Tiepolo Drawings in the Victoria and Albert
Museum,* London, 1960, cat. no. 198.   M.T.

GIOVANNI BATTISTA TIEPOLO   *Flying Female Figure,* ca. 1744

UNIVERSITY ART MUSEUM, UNIVERSITY OF CALIFORNIA,
BERKELEY. Museum No. 1968.4.
269 x 199 mm.; pen and brown ink and wash; inscribed in
an old hand, "rr" (lower left).
Collections: Count Algarotti Corniani, Venice (?); Edward
Cheney, Shrops. (?); E. Parsons and Sons, London (?);
A. Scharf, London; Paul Drey Gallery, New York.
Exhibited: The Baltimore Museum of Art, *The Age of
Elegance: The Rococo and its Effects,* 1959, cat. no. 217;
Herron Museum of Art, Indianapolis, *Old Master Drawings,*
1962, cat. no. 34.

This drawing in Tiepolo's favorite medium of pen and wash
cannot be related to any particular figure in Tiepolo's other
works. It is a simple figure of the type which Tiepolo
produced by the hundreds. They were not done from models:
in the words of Byam Shaw, ". . . the forms are not
individualized, but translated into the characteristic Tiepolo
idiom. Even the single figure studies . . . make the impression
of having been drawn by an artist devising types and

rehearsing motives . . . rather than for specific paintings or etchings."[1]

A possible provenance for this drawing may be one of the nine albums of Tiepolo drawings bought in 1852 by Edward Cheney from Count Algarotti Corniani at Venice, whose family had presumably been in possession of the drawings since Tiepolo's day. One of the Cheney albums, entitled *Sole figure per soffitti* (single figures for ceilings), was sold at Christie's July 14, 1914. It was probably bought by E. Parsons and Sons, who sold off the drawings separately after World War I.[2] A figure seen from below, as is this angel, may well have come from that album.

[1] Arts Council of Great Britain, *An Exhibition of Drawings and Etchings by Giovanni Battista and Giovanni Domenico Tiepolo,* London, 1955, 6-7. [2] G.Knox, *Tiepolo Drawings in the Victoria and Albert Museum,* London, 1960, 7.   L.O.

58:140   GIOVANNI BATTISTA TIEPOLO   *Bearded Man Wearing a Cloak and Tall Hat,* ca. 1750

SANTA BARBARA MUSEUM OF ART. GIFT OF WRIGHT LUDINGTON. Museum No. 64.12.
206 x 126 mm.; pen and brown ink and wash.
Collections: Count Algarotti Corniani, Venice (?); Edward Cheney, Shrops. (?); E. Parsons and Sons, London (?); Charles E. Slatkin Galleries, Inc., New York; Wright Ludington, Santa Barbara.
Literature: Santa Barbara Museum of Art, *European Drawings, 1450-1900,* 1964, cat. no. 78 (illus.).

59:141   GIOVANNI BATTISTA TIEPOLO   *Young Man in a Flat Cap,* ca. 1750

HUNT FOODS & INDUSTRIES MUSEUM OF ART, FULLERTON.
240 x 155 mm.; pen and brown ink and wash over pencil.
Collections: Count Algarotti Corniani, Venice (?); Edward Cheney, Shrops. (?); E. Parsons and Sons, London (?).

The strong similarity between these drawings and several other drawings of figures in the Victoria and Albert Museum, London,[1] may indicate that they are two of the missing drawings from an album entitled *Sole figure vestiti* (single dressed figures). This album of Tiepolo drawings was one of nine bought in Venice in 1852 by Edward Cheney from Count Algarotti Corniani. After Cheney's death in 1885, it was acquired along with one other album by the Victoria and Albert Museum. At that time, however, a few of its leaves were missing.

Knox dates the drawings from the *Sole figure vestiti* album as earlier than 1751 and probably ca. 1750.[2] Like the preceding study of a *Flying Female Figure* (no. 57 in the present catalogue), they are sketches of favorite motives rather than studies for any specific figures in particular paintings by Tiepolo.

[1]See G.Knox, *Tiepolo Drawings in the Victoria and Albert Museum,* London, 1960, pls. 132, 141-147, 157, 173-176, 191, 216, and 280-286, 295. [2]For his arguments, see *ibid.,* 66.
L.O.

60:143   GIOVANNI DOMENICO TIEPOLO (1727–1804)   *Pulcinella Presides at a Hanging,* after 1800

STANFORD UNIVERSITY MUSEUM. MORTIMER C. LEVENTRITT COLLECTION.
355 x 470 mm.; black chalk, pen and brown ink and wash, with dark brown and yellow washes; inscribed, "98" (upper left, recto), signed, "Dom. Tiepolo fc." (lower left, recto), inscribed, "[illegible] half only" and "Vol. o no page" (top, verso).
Collections: [sold] Sotheby's, London, 6 July 1920; E. P. Colnaghi & Sons, London; Richard Owen, Paris; Dan Fellows Platt, Englewood, N.J.; Mortimer C. Leventritt, San Francisco.
Literature: T. Welton, *The M. C. Leventritt Collection of Far Eastern and European Art,* Stanford, 1941, cat. no. 278; D. M. Mendelowitz, *Drawing,* New York, 1967, 95, figs. 4, 15. *Exhibited:* The Art Institute of Chicago, *Paintings, Drawings and Prints by the Tiepolo,* 1938, cat. no. 110.

61:144   GIOVANNI DOMENICO TIEPOLO   *Pulcinella's Last Illness,* after 1800

STANFORD UNIVERSITY MUSEUM. MORTIMER C. LEVENTRITT COLLECTION.
355 x 472 mm.; black chalk, pen and brown ink and wash, with dark brown and yellow washes; inscribed, "83" (upper left corner).
Collections: same as above.
Literature: Welton, *op.cit.,* cat. no. 277; D. C. Rich, "Laocoön and Pulcinello," *Parnassus,* 1938, X, ii, 7.
Exhibited: Chicago, *loc.cit.,* cat. no. 107.

These two sheets belong to the most celebrated series of drawings by the younger Tiepolo, the *Divertimento per li Ragazzi,* consisting altogether of 104 sheets (including the frontispiece, now in the William Rockhill Nelson Gallery in Kansas City, Missouri).[1] It was probably produced for the pleasure of the artist and his friends, although it may have

been intended for a projected but unexecuted series of
etchings. The set was placed on sale by an unknown owner
at the London auction house of Sotheby & Sons in 1920,
and was acquired soon after by a Paris collector. In 1921
the series was broken up. Nineteen of the drawings have
ended up in this country, twelve are in the collection of
Brinsley Ford at London, and the remainder are scattered
through museums and collections in Europe.[2]

All the drawings deal with Pulcinella, the famous buffoon
character of the Neapolitan *commedia dell'arte*. For
Domenico, Pulcinella seemed to symbolize a capricious and
droll humanity, while the similarly masked comrades who
attend him might be thought of as the various
personifications of Pulcinella's moods.[3] Domenico's father,
Giovanni Battista Tiepolo, produced some satirical drawings
and etched *scherzi* of Pulcinella, but it was not until
Domenico's frescoes of 1793 for the Tiepolo villa at Zianigo,
now in the Ca' Rezzonico at Venice,[4] that these whimsical,
hunchbacked figures in their bizarre costumes seemed to
take on a complete life of their own.

No clear narrative sequence has been discovered in the
series, but several have been proposed. The most plausible
is Byam Shaw's notion that the drawings fall into several
groups related in theme: ancestry; childhood and youthful
amusements of Pulcinella; trades and occupations;
adventures in strange lands; social and official life; illness
and death. Under this interpretation the first of our drawings
would belong to the fifth group and shows Pulcinella in the
role of a law official presiding at a hanging (not as the
victim on the gallows). The second drawing would show the
beginning of Pulcinella's last illness. A variation of the
latter exists.[5]

The Pulcinella drawings are rather large and are attractive
for contrasts of lights and darks, and for the playfully
patterned splotches of tone that are formed in the washes.
There is a richness of effect produced by the vivacity and
bustling assertiveness in the figure groupings, and by the
interesting detail that is often introduced. Texturally, their
effect is heightened by a marked scoring of the paper that is
especially noticeable in the dark areas of wash, and which
is even incorporated into the design of some of the drawings
in the series. Due to the artist's advanced age, however,
the character of the line has become tired and wobbly, and
one often finds a casual clumsiness in the rendering of
details. There is also a stereotyping in the figures and poses.

[1]J.Byam Shaw, *The Drawings of Domenico Tiepolo*,
London, 1962, 52 ff. [2]Byam Shaw, *op.cit.*, 52, n. 3. Ford
has also assembled a complete set of photographs of the
series, numbered according to the order in which the
drawings were originally bound into their album. The
Stanford drawings are respectively nos. 95 and 83 in this set.
The discrepancy between the first number and that actually
on the drawing may be due to an error of recording.
[3]Byam Shaw, *op.cit.*, 54 ff. Mr. Byam Shaw has been
especially helpful to the compiler of this entry by his quick
and full replies to our written inquiries. [4]T.Pignatti, *Il Museo
Correr di Venezia: dipinti del XVII e XVIII secolo*, Venice,
1960, 362-374. [5]Formerly in the collection of Léon Suzor,
Paris; Byam Shaw, *op.cit.*, 56, n. 3. It is no. 13 in Mr. Ford's
set of photographs.   M.S.

E. B. CROCKER ART GALLERY, SACRAMENTO. Museum
No. 327-13.
202 x 201 mm.; black chalk, pen and brown ink
and wash heightened with white, on blue paper (recto),
black chalk, pen and black ink (verso); inscribed in a later
hand, "Alessandro Turchi Veronese", "2J", and "No. 3287"
(verso); inscribed in a contemporary hand, "POLYMNIA
SATVRNI/le case sono acquario e capricornus/[C]opia
di memoria e [illegible]" (on a fragment of the same blue
paper pasted beneath the verso).
Exhibited: M. H. de Young Memorial Museum, San
Francisco, *Man: Glory, Jest and Riddle,* 1965, cat. no. 117.

At the left of this sheet is a seated female figure holding an
hourglass in her left hand and in her right hand an open
book. Her left hand rests on a lyre. Clearly the goat at her
feet symbolizes Capricorn, while the figure at the right
pouring water from an urn is Aquarius. Both constellations
are ruled by Saturn in conventional astrological lore.[1]
Capricorn is the male, or day house of the planet, and the
goat's head is accordingly seen in light. Aquarius is the
female, or night house, and its figure is appropriately shown
as female with the face mostly in shade. (Representations
in art of Saturn's rule over these two houses are well known,
as in an illustration in Michael Maier's *Viatorium hoc est
di Montibus Planetarum septem, feu Metallorum,*
Rouen, 1651.)
However, it is not Saturn himself that is shown in mastery,
but Polyhymnia (or Polymnia), one of the nine muses,
variously described as muse of the mimic arts, of sacred
poetry, or of sacred songs. It is in this last role, in her
relationship to music, that her identification with Saturn
becomes clear. The Renaissance concept of the Harmony of
the Universe included the notion that musical tones or modes
animate the "spheres" or planets, and that each planet was
associated with one of the nine muses. An illustration of this
notion is seen, for instance, in the woodcut frontispiece to
Franchino Gafurio's *Practica Musica,* published in Milan in
1496. There the muse Polyhymnia corresponds to the
planet Saturn.[2] The pensive, serious temperament of the
muse is associated with the saturnine traits of reticence,
perseverance and melancholy.
The allegorical meaning of this drawing therefore is this
dual harmony of Saturn and sacred poetry as made clear by
the inscription on the verso. The identification of the subject
explains the various attributes. The lyre, though not
particular to Polyhymnia, is nevertheless appropriate as
representing either music or poetry.[3] The open book may
refer to the muse, music, poetry, or perhaps even
melancholy.[4] The hourglass is a conventional attribute of
Saturn, and alludes generally to the passage of time,
approaching death, and melancholy.[5] The concepts of time
and death recur in the scythe (attribute of Saturn as alter
ego to Cronos) which lies on the ground between the figures
of Capricorn and Aquarius.[6] In the left background is what
appears to be a headless herma pilaster and part of an arch.

It is not clear whether this is merely a compositional motive or has some other significance. The purpose of this drawing is likewise unclear. It may be the *modello* for a painted emblem, a grisaille panel, or a temporary (perhaps funerary) decoration. The figure on the verso is presumably another version of Polyhymnia. What the "copy from memory" is, referred to in the inscription, remains unknown.

[1]G.de Tervarent, *Attributs et symboles dans l'art profane 1450-1600,* Geneva, 1958, cols. 60, 401. [2]J.Seznec, *The Survival of the Pagan Gods,* New York, 1953, 140, fig. 48. [3]Tervarent, *op.cit.,* cols. 256f. [4]*Ibid.,* cols. 249 ff. [5]*Ibid.,* cols. 220, 329 ff. [6]*Ibid.,* cols. 164f.   M.S.

63:147   NICLAES BERCHEM (1620–1683)   *Travelers on a Forest Road*

ACHENBACH FOUNDATION FOR GRAPHIC ARTS, CALIFORNIA PALACE OF THE LEGION OF HONOR, SAN FRANCISCO. 302 x 235 mm.; trimmed (?); torn upper right corner; black chalk and grey wash. *Collections:* Henry M. Mitchell, Hydra, Greece.

Niclaes Berchem belongs to the second generation of the so-called Dutch-Italianate landscape painters. He went to Rome in 1642 where he stayed for three years. He might have made another trip to Italy in the 1650's, judging from his dated drawings of that decade which represent Campagna landscapes with ruins.[1] After his return to Holland, Berchem treated Italian motives in combination with the Dutch landscape. Together with Tassi, Sandrart and Claude, he was one of the few artists who drew directly from nature at that time. A majority of his finished drawings, however, were done later in his own studio from sketches he had made outdoors. Since Berchem repeatedly used the same types of figures, animals and settings, it is very difficult to date his compositions. For example, the woman seated almost playfully on the horse appears in numerous drawings and paintings dated from the 1640's through the 1660's. The fact that he signed "Berghem" on the works up to around 1655 and "Berchem" on later works provides a clue for signed works, of which, however, this is not one. It is tempting to place the Achenbach drawing in the 1650's, based on its openness and shimmering atmosphere. After that time Dutch landscape in general shows a "return to structure," in which tall trees play an important architectonic role.[2]

[1]I.von Sick, *Nicolaes Berchem: Ein Voläufer des Rokoko,* dissertation, Köln, 1929, 32. [2]W.Stechow, *Dutch Landscape Paintings of the 17th Century,* 32.   S.H.

E. B. CROCKER ART GALLERY, SACRAMENTO. Museum
No. 114-1.
312 x 184 mm.; upper left corner torn, small tear at
upper right edge; pen and brown ink.
Collections: Edwin Crocker, Sacramento.
Exhibited: E. B. Crocker Art Gallery, Sacramento, *The
Bible As Seen by the Old Masters,* 1941, cat. no. 33.

This composition of a saint meditating over an open prayer
book while surrounded by monsters, is very similar to
Temptation scenes by Bosch. The scene is set in a northern
landscape of abrupt mounds, water and stumpy trees.
A swarm of grotesque figures is trying to distract the hermit
who bears the 'T' of Saint Anthony on his right shoulder.
The composition in superimposed zones without a clear
recession into depth is also in the manner of Bosch. So are
the individual landscape motives and hybrid beings (half
man, half beast) who represent the vanity of the world and
the vices of mankind. The laid table at the left and the man
pouring wine into a bowl stand for gluttony. To the right,
the nun with a jug on her head playing the harp alludes to
the corrupt clergy. Fish and shield are symbols of lust.[1]
The monster types are nearest to the demons of Bosch's late
period. None of them, however, can be identified as specific
models for monsters in any known works of Bosch.
Comparing this sheet with the master's known sketches of
monsters, it is apparent that these monsters are less
zoomorphic than those of Bosch and that few of them sport
wings, such as Bosch himself liked to provide.[2] The technique
with which the monsters are drawn does not correspond
to the manner of Bosch either: the lines are longer, more
fluid and more regular. The discrepancy becomes even more
obvious if we compare this sheet to the master's only
generally accepted sketch of a *Temptation,* in Berlin.[3] The
same differences come to light in the treatment of the tree or
in the abbreviations for hand and feet. The drawings in the
Bosch corpus that are closest to the Sacramento sheet are
significantly those of most dubious authenticity.[4] The design
of the composition seems to be directly inspired by Bosch
(perhaps by a lost *Temptation*), but the style is translated
into the language of the late sixteenth century. It is possible
that the draughtsman was Pieter Bruegel the Younger, who
is known to have used Bosch sketches as models.[5]

[1]C.de Tolnay, *Hieronymus Bosch,* Baden-Baden, 1966, 27-28,
357-358. [2]*Ibid.,* cat. nos. 12, 16, 17. [3]*Ibid.,* cat. no. 5. [4]*Ibid.,*
cat. nos. 9, 11v. [5]*Ibid.,* cat. nos. 10a, 14a. Charles de Tolnay
in a letter to the compiler has suggested the drawing might
be closer in time to the age of Bosch, and perhaps be a
work of Jan de Cock.   E.G.

E. B. CROCKER ART GALLERY, SACRAMENTO. Museum
No. 150-21.
324 x 311 mm.; black chalk, pen and brown ink and
wash; inscribed with the artist's monogram[1] and date,
"Ano 1627" (lower right), and in the same hand, "Tempio
della Sybilla/Tiburtina a Tivoli" (bottom right).
Collections: Baron C. Rolas du Rosey, Leipzig (Lugt 2237);
Edwin Crocker, Sacramento.
Literature: R. Weigel, *Weigel's Kunstkatalog,* Leipzig, 1838,
I, no. 1108; N. Trivas, *Old Master Drawings from the E. B.
Crocker Collection: The Dutch and Flemish Masters,* no. 17.
Exhibited: E. B. Crocker Art Gallery, Sacramento, *Three
Centuries of Landscape Drawing,* 1940, cat. no. 25.

The drawing represents the now partly restored Temple of
Vesta in Tivoli, believed in previous centuries to have been a
temple of the Tiburtine Sibyl.[2] It is a monopteron standing
on the cliff overlooking the famous cascades. Of eighteen
Corinthian columns, ten are still standing. In the Crocker
drawing the temple is seen from the south and fills almost
the entire height of the sheet.
Breenbergh belongs to the first generation of the so-called
Dutch-Italianate landscape painters. He is said to have
worked in Italy with Poelenburgh and both of them were
influenced by Adam Elsheimer and Paul Brill (whose works
were copied by Breenbergh many times). A majority of
Breenbergh's dated drawings fall in the ten years of his
Roman period, 1620-1629, and particularly between 1625
and 1627.[3] The drawings of the year 1627 show the artist
especially interested in the effects of light. They include
numerous pen-and-wash drawings of the ruins in Rome and
the Campagna, clothed in strong sunlight and transparent
shadows.
There are two more known drawings of the same subject
by Breenbergh, in the Dresden printroom[4] and in The
Pierpont Morgan Library, New York.[5] The Temple of Vesta
in Tivoli was one of the favorite subjects of northern
European artists in Italy, from the time of Marten van
Heemskerck, who visited Rome in 1532-1538, down to the
time of Hubert Robert (at Rome 1754-1765) and later.[6]

[1]Nagler, *Monogrammisten,* no. 1701. [2]T.Pignatore, *The
Ancient Monuments of Rome,* London, 1932, 102. Inv. no.
1898-30. [3]G.Naumann, *Die Landschaftszeichnungen des
Bartholomeus Breenbergh,* dissertation, Heidelberg, 1933, 5.
[4]Naumann, *loc.cit.* [5]C.Fairfax Murray, *Drawings by the
Old Masters, Collection of J.Pierpont Morgan,* London,
1905-1912, III, no. 212. [6]See C.Hülsen and H.Egger, *Die
Römischer Skizzenbücher von Marten van Heemskerck,*
Berlin, 1913-1916, I, fol. 21r; G.K.Loukomski and P.de
Nolhac, *La Roma d'Hubert Robert,* Paris, 1930, pls. 75,
76.   S.H.

SANTA BARBARA MUSEUM OF ART. Museum No. 59.40.
162 x 352 mm.; torn center bottom (repaired); black chalk
and colored washes.

Pieter Bruegel the Younger is best known for his numerous
copies and variants of compositions by his father, Pieter
Bruegel the Elder. Although no other landscape drawings by
him are identical with this one, the attribution is strongly
supported by stylistic comparison with his representations of
other subjects. The carefully rendered rusticity of the
farmhouses and the use of shadow and decorative
draughtsmanship in the trees are very close to a signed
Peasant Wedding, sold at Christie's on 20 March 1964.[1]
A drawing in the British Museum of a *Peasant Wedding and
Dance,* incorporating motives copied from a drawing by
(and a print after) Pieter Bruegel the Elder, is similar to
the present drawing in the careful handling of wash, the
distribution of shadows, and the decorative stippling used to
render thatched roofs.[2]

[1]Illus., *Burlington Magazine,* 1964, CVI, advertising
supplement for March, xvii. [2]L.Münz, *Bruegel: Die
Zeichnungen,* 1962, cat. no. A-49.   D.A.

67:151   HENDRIK GOLTZIUS (1558–1617)   *The Artist's Emblem,* 1609

E. B. CROCKER ART GALLERY, SACRAMENTO. Museum
No. 143-2.
150 x 89 mm.; pen and brown ink; inscribed by the
artist, "EER BOVEN GOLT." (top) and "A° 1609"
(bottom). Signed with his monogram (on the urn).[1]
Literature: E. K. J. Reznicek, *Die Zeichnungen von Henrick
Goltzius,* Utrecht, 1961, I, 316, cat. no. 197, II, 428.
Exhibited: E. B. Crocker Art Gallery, Sacramento, *Ten
Problems—Nine Solutions,* 1940, cat. no. 5; *idem, The Bible
As Seen by the Old Masters,* 1941, cat. no. 14.

This drawing is one of five known pictorial representations
of the artist's motto: "Honor Above Gold."[2] The goblets
and the vessels with coins, as well as the caduceus (symbol
of trade), represent gold. The rays and the cherub head
crowned with a laurel wreath represent honor. The emblem
may be read from top to bottom as meaning honor ranks
above wealth acquired by trade. Interpreted in reverse, it
means wealth and gain may lead to honorable liberality.
Goltzius was known for his generosity.[3] The emblem also
contains a rebus, which is made explicit in two of the
representations by punning on the first four letters of the
artist's last name, *Golt*zius.[4]
All representations follow the same iconography. There are

only some slight changes in the position of the sun and in the symbols of wealth which are variously a treasure box, silver cups, a golden chain, heaps of coins, or a money bag. In one drawing Goltzius adds to the emblem two allegorical figures and depicts compasses and a justifier in the foreground.[5] These additions give a third connotation to the emblem and to the meaning of the cherub floating in the sky: 'Money can make a merchant but never an artist' — a dictum of the master recorded by Carel van Mander.[6] Two of the other drawings of this emblem were part of a *Liber Amicorum* and probably the present sheet served a similar purpose. The technical virtuosity and hard, precise drawing relate clearly to the master's activity as an engraver. This sheet, which seems to be the latest of the pen drawings in this series, displays an unusual concern with pictorial effects such as light and shade. It reflects Goltzius' growing experience at the time in painting.

[1]Nagler, *Monogrammisten,* III, no. 952. [2]Reznicek, *op.cit.,* cat. nos. 195, 196, 198, and emblem in cartouche under the portrait of Goltzius engraved by J.Matham (B. 23, Ho. 379). [3]Reznicek, *op.cit.,* 201. [4]*Ibid.,* cat. no. 195, and the cited engraving by J.Matham. [5]Reznicek, *op.cit.,* cat. no. 198. [6]*Het Schilderboek,* ed. Amsterdam, 1936, 500.   E.G.

68:152   MARTEN VAN HEEMSKERCK (1498–1574)   *Joseph and Potiphar's Wife,* 1566

ACHENBACH FOUNDATION FOR GRAPHIC ARTS, CALIFORNIA PALACE OF THE LEGION OF HONOR, SAN FRANCISCO. 210 x 260 mm.; small holes in upper left and right corners; pen and brown ink; signed and dated, "M. Heemskerck 1566" (lower right).
Collections: Sir Robert Witt, London; George E. Hume, San Francisco.
Literature: J. MacAgy, "Six Ecclesiastical Drawings from the Museum Collections," *Bulletin of the California Palace of the Legion of Honor,* 1954, XII: 8, no page number (illus.). *Exhibited:* Pomona College Gallery, Claremont, California, *Mannerism,* 1963; The John and Mable Ringling Museum of Art, Sarasota, Florida, *Master Drawings,* 1967.

The rather dry penmanship of this drawing indicates that it, like most surviving Heemskerck figure compositions, was a preparatory study for an engraving. Heemskerck twice illustrated the story of Joseph fleeing from the advances of Potiphar's wife (Genesis 39:12). The first time was in a series of six engravings of the life of Joseph, dated 1549 and 1550.[1] He returned to the theme again in the 1560's in a series of ten prints of the Ten Commandments, each depicted by an appropriate incident. The ninth commandment, "Thou shalt not bear false witness," was illustrated with the story of Joseph and Potiphar's wife.[2] This drawing is apparently a study for that print. Another drawing for the series, also signed and dated 1566, depicting the story of Cain and Abel (the subject chosen for the sixth commandment), is still in the Witt Collection, now owned by the Courtauld Institute of Art in London.[3]

The conception of the scene, with its shallow planar composition and its action proceeding vigorously toward the right, is typical of the northern iconographic tradition and is comparable with a print of the same subject by Lucas van Leyden of 1512.[4] However, the use of the elongated nude figure, the elaborately contrived poses and the archeological accuracy of the costumes and furnishings reveal Heemskerck as a mannerist attempting to combine northern precision of detail with an Italianate classicism.

[1]T.Kerrich, *A Catalogue of Prints Which Have Been Engraved after Marten van Heemskerck; or Rather an Essay Toward Such a Catalogue,* Cambridge, 1829, 13-14; F.W.H.Hollstein, *Dutch and Flemish Etchings, Engravings and Woodcuts ca. 1450-1700,* Amsterdam, n.d., VIII, 238, nos. 46-51. [2]Kerrich, *op.cit.,* 4-5; Hollstein, *op.cit.,* VIII, 246, no. 400. [3]Courtauld Institute of Art, London University, *Handlist of the Drawings in the Witt Collection,* 1956, no. 3897. [4]Hollstein, *op.cit.,* X, 73.   K.T.

69:153   PETER PAUL RUBENS (1577–1640)   *Head of a Bearded Man*

E. B. CROCKER ART GALLERY, SACRAMENTO. Museum No. 219-23.
330 x 277 mm.; horizontal folds, black and white chalk; inscribed in a later hand, "P. P. Rubbens fect" (lower left, recto), "P. P. Rubbens P./geb. Keulen 1577/b. 13d./b. 11.d/No. 2—" and "Herrn Rudolf Weigel innigster und aufrichtigster Dankbarkeit. Herman Weber in Bonn" (pasted to mount, verso).
Collections: Herman Weber, Bonn; Rudolph Weigel, Leipzig; Edwin Crocker, Sacramento. *Exhibited:* E. B. Crocker Art Gallery, Sacramento, *Drawings of the Masters,* 1959 (illus.).

Rubens has built up with remarkably sure strokes this impressive, powerfully concrete visage. The unruly hair gives a lively impression to the head, as does the suggestion of movement created by the slightly different directions of head and body. For Rubens, a drawing was seldom an end in itself. Most of his studies of heads for particular paintings consist of basic outlines and spare modeling, and often have additional studies of arms, hands and even other heads on the same sheet.[1] This head could be a portrait and in fact the collar is of a contemporary fashion, but it conforms to a facial type common in Rubens' paintings. Certainly the master often idealized his sitters according to certain types,[2] but most of his obvious portrait drawings are in full face or three-quarter view, not in profile perdu.[3]

[1]J.S.Held, *Rubens Drawings,* New York, 1959, cat. nos. 77, 79, 89, 96; L.Burchard and R.A.d'Hulst, *Rubens Drawings,* Brussels, 1963, cat. nos. 75, 111, 121, 146v, 157; G.Glück

and F.M.Haberditzl, *Die Handzeichnungen Peter Paul Rubens,* Berlin, 1928, cat. nos. 142, 169, 206. ²For example, witness the transformation of Rubens' wife between the chalk study (F.Lugt, *Musée du Louvre Inventaire général des dessins des écoles du nord école flamand,* Paris, 1949, cat. no. 1032, pl. 30) and the painted portrait (R.Oldenberg, *Peter Paul Rubens: Des Meisters Gemälde,* Stuttgart [Klassiker der Kunst], 1921, V, 424). ³Lugt, *op.cit.,* cat. no. 1019; Burchard and d'Hulst, *op.cit.,* cat. nos. 170, 171, 201, 202; Held, *op.cit.,* cat. nos. 126, 139.   W.W.

70:154   ROELANT SAVERY (1576–1639)   *Elephants and a Monkey*

E. B. CROCKER ART GALLERY, SACRAMENTO. Museum No. 101-22.
138 x 210 mm.; black chalk and brown wash; signed, "SAVERY/EE" (on the stone, bottom center).
Collections: C. Rolas du Rosey, Dresden (Lugt 2237); Jungmeister; Edwin Crocker, Sacramento.
Literature: J. Bialostocki, "Les bêtes et les humains de Roelant Savery," *Bulletin Koniklijke Musea voor Schoone Kunsten,* 1958, no. 2, 87. *Exhibited:* Musée des Beaux-Arts, Ghent, *Roelant Savery,* 1954, cat. no. 108.

71:155   ROELANT SAVERY   *Dodo Birds*

E. B. CROCKER ART GALLERY, SACRAMENTO. Museum No. 102-22.
138 x 210 mm.; black chalk and brown wash; signed, "SAVERY" (lower left).
Collections: same as above.
Literature: J. Bialostocki, "Les bêtes et les humains de Roelant Savery," *Bulletin Koniklijke Musea voor Schoone Kunsten,* 1958, no. 2, 87; H. Freidman, "New Light on the Dodo and its Illustrators," *Smithsonian Report,* 1956, publication no. 4250, 475-481; E. K. C. Reznicek, *Die Zeichnungen von Hendrick Goltzius,* Utrecht, 1961, I, 207. *Exhibited:* Musée des Beaux-Arts, Ghent, *Roelant Savery,* 1954, cat. no. 107.

These animal studies probably were made in the famous *Vivarium* of Prague during Savery's employment at the court of the Emperor Rudolf II, 1604-1613. In accordance with the widespread interest in natural history at that time, the Emperor imported rare animals from distant countries and kept painters in his service to portray them. In this capacity Savery carried on the work of his compatriots Georg and Jacob Hoefnagel.

There exists another somewhat larger drawing of an elephant in the Albertina and a drawing depicting a monkey is preserved in the Rijksprentenkabinet in Amsterdam.[1] Savery made extensive use of his life studies in his paintings, and these elephants appear again in several of his works, e.g., the *Garden of Eden* and *Orpheus Charming the Animals* in Vienna. The motive of a monkey sitting on an elephant occurs in a Savery picture at Warsaw of *Noah's Ark*.[2] The second drawing is of special interest to the natural historian as a record of the extinct species *Dronte Didus Ineptus*.[3] The master seems to be at greater ease depicting the short, winged, plump bodies of these birds than the monumental immensity of an elephant. In his flower pieces Savery tends to dramatize the birds, frogs and insects that he introduces, by showing them in conflict.[4] Here too, the birds seem to be fighting one another. Just as in the case of the elephants, Savery repeated the birds in other works. A life-size picture of a dodo is in the Natural History Department of the British Museum, and several dodos figure in the Vienna *Orpheus* and in a *Landscape with Birds* in the same museum.[5]

Both drawings are related in size, style of signature, and technique to some studies of stags, eagles and camels, and probably derive from the same sketchbook.[6] Although some scholars maintain that Savery's interest in animals dates from a later period, and although his pictures depicting dodos date from the 1620's, it is likely that the Sacramento drawings were made during Savery's first years in Prague, in 1604-1605.[7] The composition in two planes, the scene-like use of trees and the detailed execution of the animals are all characteristic features of his early work. Exotic shells such as appear here (probably rare specimens from the Emperor's *Wunderkammer*) also appear in the foreground of a *Landscape with Tobias and the Angel,* signed and dated "PRAGA 1605."[8]

[1] K.Erasmus, *Roelant Savery,* Halle, 1908, cat. no. 189.
[2] J. Bialostocki, *op.cit.,* 74, fig. 4. [3] K.Erasmus, *op.cit.,* 47.
[4] I.Bergstrom, *Dutch Still Life Painting,* London, 1956, 91-93.
[5] K.Erasmus, *op.cit.,* cat. nos. 17, 64, 113, 154. [6] *Ibid.,* cat. nos. 3, 9, 49. [7] *Ibid.,* 36, 49, 149; A.Laer, "Le peintre courtraisien, Roelant Savery," *Revue belge d'archéologie et d'histoire de l'art,* 1931, 320. [8] K.Erasmus, *op.cit.,* cat. no. 179. E.G.

72:158 JAN VAN DER STRAET, CALLED JOANNES STRADANUS (1523-1605) *Title Page for Homer's "Odyssey"*

ACHENBACH FOUNDATION FOR GRAPHIC ARTS, CALIFORNIA PALACE OF THE LEGION OF HONOR, SAN FRANCISCO. 211 x 305 mm.; torn vertically and repaired; pen and brown ink, blue and brown wash heightened with white; signed, "ioannes/stradanus" (on the book, bottom right), inscribed by the artist, "titola Arme musa," and "NavigAzatione di Ulisse da Luj narate Alla cenna/del Re Alcinoo nj corfu/Cauata da Homero—" (below the margin).

Collections: Joseph Green Cogswell; Mortimer L. Schiff;
Moore S. Achenbach, San Francisco.
Literature: Hellman, *Original Drawings,* cat. no. 245.

A drawing of *Circe Changing the Companions of Ulysses
into Animals* is at Windsor Castle.[1] It is similar stylistically
to the Achenbach drawing and is related in theme. However,
no printed edition of Homer's *Odyssey* illustrated by
Stradanus is known to the compiler.
Born in Bruges, Flanders, in 1523, Stradanus received his
artistic training in his native city and in Antwerp. After
civil strife broke out in Flanders he left for Italy in 1550
and established himself in Florence.[2] From there he
continued to supply engravers in Munich and Antwerp with
drawings. Often they are annotated with explanatory notes
for the instruction of the engraver.[3]
This sheet dates from the end of Stradanus' career, when
the swirling placement of figures from his mannerist period
is replaced with a clear spatial relationship between figures
and setting in the style of the Florentine Renaissance.

[1]L.van Puyvelde, *The Flemish Drawings . . . at Windsor
Castle,* London, 1942, cat. no. 167. [2]For a discussion of
Stradanus' early career and work in Italy, see G.Thiem,
"Studien zu Jan van der Straet, genannt Stradanus,"
Mitteilungen des Kunsthistorisches Institut in Florenz, 1958,
VIII, 188-211. [3]M.N.Benisovich, "The Drawings of Stradanus
(Jan van der Straet) in the Cooper Union Museum," *The
Art Bulletin,* 1956, XXXVIII, 249, and Thiem, *op.cit.,* 92,
n. 18.   M.T.

73:156   HERMAN VAN SWANEVELT (CA. 1600–1655)   *Landscape with Fauns,* 1639

E. B. CROCKER ART GALLERY, SACRAMENTO. Museum
No. 159-3.
203 x 262 mm.; trimmed slightly all around; red
chalk, pen and brown ink and wash, and grey wash; signed,
"HvSwanevelt fa. Roma/1639" (below the tree trunk, lower
left).
Collections: Edwin Crocker, Sacramento.
Exhibited: E. B. Crocker Art Gallery, Sacramento, *Three
Centuries of Landscape Drawing,* 1940, cat. no. 24.

The signature and date make the present drawing an
interesting document for tracing the career of a still shadowy
personality. Traditionally, Swanevelt was thought to have
come to Rome in the later 1620's and to have left in 1638,
the last year he was mentioned in the proceedings of the
Academy of Saint Luke.[1] But the inscription here shows that
he was still in Rome in 1639. Recently another drawing has
been recorded, signed and dated at Rome in 1641, proving
his continued presence there for two more years.[2]
The Crocker drawing is important not only as a biographical
but also as a stylistic document. Only two signed and dated
paintings by the artist are known, and only three dated

drawings besides the Crocker drawing are from Swanevelt's Roman period.[3] In these years he completed the transition, begun by Poelenburgh and Breenbergh, between the earlier group of Dutch landscapists in Rome (the Pynas brothers, Lastman, Goudt and Brill) and the later "Italianate" group headed by Jan Both, with whom Swanevelt is often confused. In this process he many times paralleled Claude Lorrain, with whom he sketched after nature in the Roman Campagna.[4] By the end of the 1630's, that is, by the time of the Crocker drawing, he had become very much dependent on the French artist. In the 1640's Swanevelt moved to Paris where, through paintings and etchings, he helped to popularize the Italianate style of landscape in northern Europe. Many features of his mature landscape style are already present in the Crocker drawing: the horizontal streaks of light upon the ground, the sunlit mound in the foreground with the middleground falling away into shadow, the Poelenburghian grotto, the grandly scaled trees, the tender foliage, rich with the detail of many minute leaves, the soft surfaces of the geological structures, and the haze above the distant hills. The figures with their elongated rhythm are also typical.[5]

The figures who inhabit this bucolic world are not human but satyr-fauns and nymphs, woodland deities symbolic of the fruitfulness of nature. The fact that there are no human habitations visible may reflect a personal inclination of the artist, who was nicknamed the Hermit.[6] Swanevelt peopled several other landscapes with satyrs. During the 1650's in Paris he etched a set of four landscapes with satyrs, one of which is arranged similarly to the Crocker drawing.[7] Drawings for these prints are now in the Uffizi.[8] Another drawing, of almost the same size as the Sacramento sheet and of the same subject as the mentioned etching, is now in the British Museum.[9]

[1] U.Thieme and F.Becker, *Allgemeines Lexikon der Bildenden Künstler,* Leipzig, 1907-1950, s.v. Swanevelt, 1938, XXXII, 340. [2] Courtauld Institute of Art, London University, *Handlist of the Drawings in the Witt Collection,* 1956, no. 4483. [3] M.R.Waddington, "Herman van Swanevelt in Rome," *Paragone,* 1960, XI, no. 121, 37 ff. [4] J.von Sandrart, *Deutsche Akademie,* ed. A.R.Peltzer, Munich, 1925, 190. [5] A figure very similar to the standing nymph in the Crocker drawing is seen already in a 1632 drawing at Windsor (illus., W.Bernt, *Die niederländischen Zeichner des 17. Jahrhunderts,* Munich, 1958, I, no. 558). [6] Sandrart, *op.cit.,* 190. [7] A.Bartsch, *Peintre graveur,* II, no. 52; A.von Wurzbach, *Niederländisches Künstler-lexikon,* Vienna and Leipzig, 1906-1911, II, 681, no. 52. [8] Galleria degli Uffizi, Gabinetto Disegni e Stampe, Florence, *Mostra di disegni fiamminghi e olandesi,* 1964, cat. no. 84. [9] A.M.Hind, *Catalogue of Drawings of Dutch and Flemish Artists,* British Museum, London, 1931, IV, no. 11; the drawing also relates to still another etching by the artist: Bartsch, *op.cit.,* no. 25; Wurzbach, *op.cit.,* no. 25.   S.K.

THE LOS ANGELES COUNTY MUSEUM OF ART. Museum No. 65.14.
210 x 283 mm.; pen and brown ink with grey wash.
Collections: Dr. A. Welcker; W. R. Jeudwine; Nathan Chaikin.
Exhibited: Alpine Club Gallery, London, 1964.

The presence of man is barely noticed in this forest scene which dwarfs the solitary human wanderer in the allée of trees on the left, and almost swallows the oarsman of the small boat near the castle on the right. These human accents serve only to give scale to the artist's main interest — the twisting luxuriant forest vegetation that fills most of the surface. The interest in this kind of enveloping forest scene derives from the landscapes of Gillis van Coninxloo and his circle. Many of the elements composing such landscapes are present here: the two unrelated recessions, one shadowy and hemmed in by trees, the other open and sunlit; the dark, twisting trees silhouetted against a lighter middle-ground; the rushes, fallen branch, jagged tree stump and sinuous tree roots. Natural forces pervade the scene, causing the ground to swell, the trees to writhe, the trunks to snap, and light to flicker through the foliage.

The drawing was recently acquired with the attribution to Valckenborch, a Flemish artist with few known works, who, like Gillis van Coninxloo, moved from Antwerp to Germany during the period of religious wars in the Netherlands. Similarities between this landscape and one in the Albertina signed and dated 1597, support the attribution.[1] The Albertina drawing, together with one in the Museum Plantin-Moretus at Antwerp,[2] and others that have appeared in exhibitions and sales catalogues,[3] show similarly writhing tree trunks and similar shading of foliage and earth with wash and curved parallel hatching. The serpentine movement of trunks and branches must have appealed to Valckenborch, who specialized in fantastic, agitated paintings of tournaments, shipwrecks, battles, burning cities and midnight rites in forest chapels.[4]

[1]Staatliche Graphische Sammlung Albertina, Vienna, *Die Zeichnungen der niederländischen Schulen,* 1928, cat. no. 312. Professor E.Haverkamp-Begemann has kindly communicated his agreement with the attribution, by letter to the compiler. [2]Museum Plantin-Moretus, Antwerp, *Catalogue des dessins anciens* (Brussels), 1938, cat. no. 129. [3]C.G.Boerner (firm), Düsseldorf, *Lagerliste Nr. 44,* 1966, no. 100; Rijksprentenkabinet, Amsterdam, *Verzameling R.A.Welcker,* 1956, I, cat. no. 123; Kunstalle, Bremen, and Kunsthaus, Zürich, *Handzeichnungen alter Meister aus schweizer Privatbesitz,* 1967, cat. no. 138. [4]A.Pigler, "Zum Werk des Frederick van Valckenborch," *Oud Holland,* 1962, LXXVII, 127-128; G.F.Faggini, "De broeders Frederick en Gillis van Valckenborch," Museum Boymans-van Beunigen, Rotterdam, *Bulletin,* 1963, XIV, 2 ff.   W.W.

The Passing of the Angel of Death

HENRY FUSELI (1741–1825)

Madame de Pompadour with her Daughter, Alexandrine d'Etiolles

FRANCOIS GUERIN (BEFORE 1751–AFTER 1791)

Scipio and his Son with the Envoys of Antiochus

JEAN AUGUSTE DOMINIQUE INGRES

Skater Pushing a High-Backed Sleigh

NICOLAS LANCRET (1690–1745)

The Chessplayer

ERNEST MEISSONIER (1815–1891)

Landscape with Ruins

PIERRE PATEL, THE ELDER (CA. 1620–1676)

Portrait of a Nobleman

FRANCOIS QUESNEL (1543 / 1544–1619)

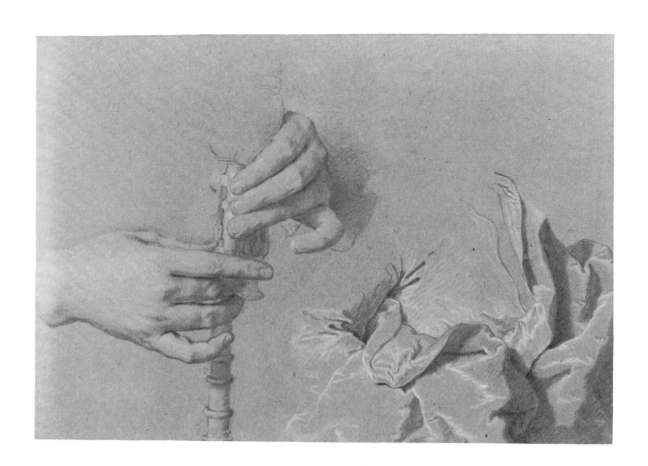

Saint Bernard of Clairvaux

PIERRE SUBLEYRAS (1699–1749), STYLE OF

20:29
96 *An Actress Dressed as Folly*

ANTOINE WATTEAU (1684–1721)

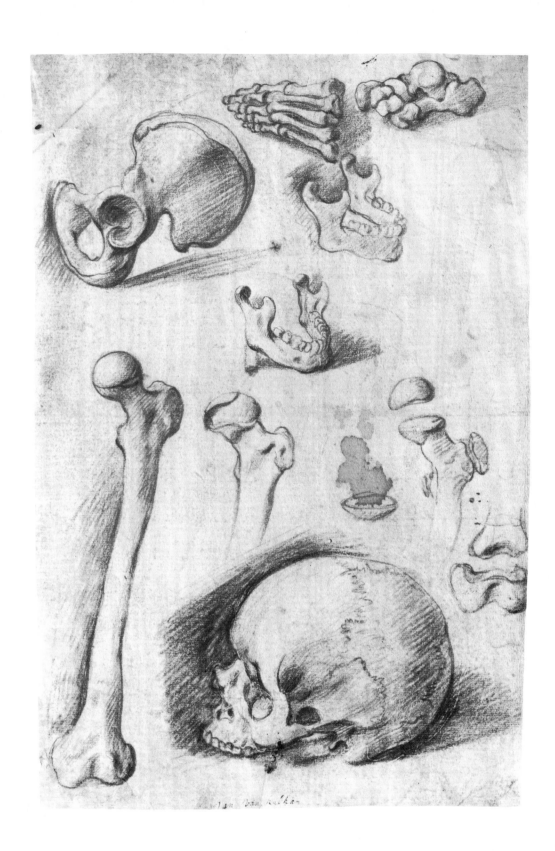

A Hip Bone, Portions of Foot, Ankle and Leg Bones, Jaws and a Skull

JAN STEFAN VAN CALCAR (1499–1546/1550)

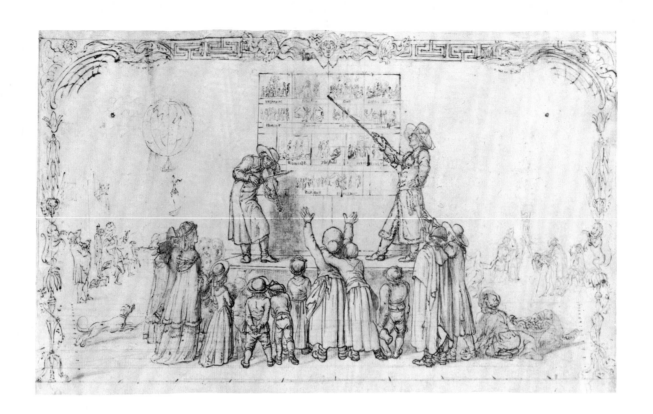

David with the Head of Goliath

GIOVANNI FRANCESCO BARBIERI, CALLED GUERCINO (1591–1666)

King David

GIOVANNI FRANCESCO BARBIERI, CALLED GUERCINO

Descent from the Cross

DOMENICO BECCAFUMI (1486–1551)

Capriccio of the Paduan Scene

BERNARDO BELLOTTO (1720–1780)

Landscape with Seated Figures in Foreground

REMIGIO CANTAGALLINA (CA. 1582–CA. 1635)

Queen Margherita of Spain Arranging the Marriage of King Sigismund of Poland with her Sister, Constanza

JACOPO CHIMENTI, CALLED JACOPO DA EMPOLI (CA. 1554–1640)

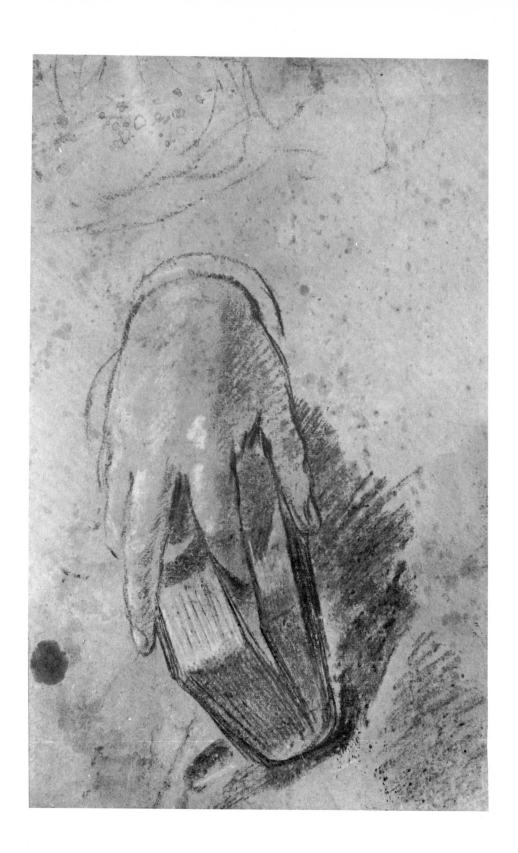

recto: *Study of a Hand Holding a Book*

ANNIBALE CARRACCI (1560–1609)

recto: *Landscape with Punting Boatman*

ANNIBALE CARRACCI

Paul farinati   E.G.   C.G.

36:43   recto: *A Bishop Making an Offering of Bread and Wine*

116   PAOLO FARINATO (CA. 1524–AFTER 1606)

Caricature of a Gentleman

PIER LEONE GHEZZI (1674–1755)

38:44 *Capriccio*

119 FRANCESCO GUARDI (1712–1793)

The Doge of Venice Receiving Ambassadors in the Sala del Collegio

FRANCESCO GUARDI, CIRCLE OF

Study for a Mural Decoration

GIOVANNI LANFRANCO (1582–1647)

Three Figures in Ecstasy

JACOPO NEGRETTI, CALLED PALMA GIOVANE (1544–1628)

45:50   *A Sea Monster*

126   GIULIO PIPPI, CALLED GIULIO ROMANO (1499–1546)

Woman on Horseback

FRANCESCO DA PONTE, CALLED BASSANO (CA. 1549–1592)

48:53   *Head of an Old Man*

129   MATTIA PRETI (1613–1699)

50:55   *A Saint Transported on a Cloud*

131   SEBASTIANO RICCI (1659–1734)

Seated Female Figure

　LUCA SIGNORELLI (CA. 1450–1523)

recto: *Female Figure with Flying Drapery and Raised Arms*

PELLEGRINO TIBALDI (1527–1596)

verso: *Female Figure with Flying Drapery and Raised Arms, a Male Head, and Figure Sketches*

PELLEGRINO TIBALDI

recto: *The Crucifixion*

GIOVANNI BATTISTA TIEPOLO

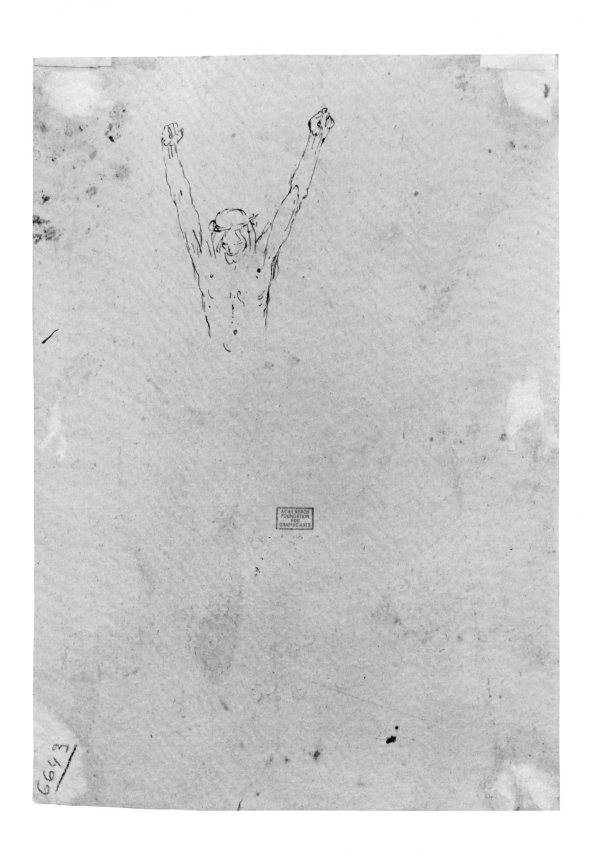

56v:61   verso: *Torso for the Figure of the Crucified Christ*

139   GIOVANNI BATTISTA TIEPOLO

Bearded Man Wearing a Cloak and Tall Hat

GIOVANNI BATTISTA TIEPOLO

Flying Female Figure

GIOVANNI BATTISTA TIEPOLO

60:63   *Pulcinella Presides at a Hanging*

143   GIOVANNI DOMENICO TIEPOLO (1727–1804)

verso: *Study for the Figure of Polymnia-Saturn*

ALESSANDRO TURCHI (1590–1649)

recto: *An Allegory of the Saturnine Muse*

ALESSANDRO TURCHI, CALLED L'ORBETTO

Travelers on a Forest Road

NICLAES BERCHEM (1620–1683)

Studies for a Temptation of Saint Anthony

HIERONYMUS BOSCH, FOLLOWER OF

Farmhouses on a Stream

PIETER BRUEGEL THE YOUNGER (1564–AFTER 1636 / 1638)

EER BOVEN GOLT.

A° 1609.

Joseph and Potiphar's Wife

MARTEN VAN HEEMSKERCK (1498–1574)

69:71 *Head of a Bearded Man*

153 PETER PAUL RUBENS (1577–1640)

Elephants and a Monkey

ROELANT SAVERY (1576–1639)

Landscape with Fauns

HERMAN VAN SWANEVELT (CA. 1600–1655)

74:76   *Landscape with Three Foreground Trees*

157   FREDERICK VAN VALCKENBORCH (1566–1623)

Navigatione d'Ulisse da La nauate Alla cenna
del Re Alcinoo in corfu
Cantata da Homero

162

163

INDEX OF LENDERS

PHOTOGRAPH CREDITS

RON CHAMBERLAIN, BERKELEY: *5, 8, 14, 17, 22, 23, 24, 25, 26, 28, 32, 32v, 35, 36, 36v, 42, 43, 46, 47, 50, 51, 57, 62, 62v, 64, 65, 67, 69, 70, 71, 73.*

JOE SCHOPPLEIN, SAN FRANCISCO: *3, 12, 13, 16, 18, 21, 29, 39, 40, 41, 45, 49, 55, 56, 56v, 63, 68, 72.*

GORDON SOMMERS, LOS ANGELES: *44.*

STANFORD UNIVERSITY PHOTOGRAPHIC DEPARTMENT, STANFORD: *7.*

Italic numbers refer to catalogue numbers used in this book.

5000 copies of this catalogue designed by Bruce Montgomery, San Francisco, have been printed in May, 1968 on the occasion of the exhibition, MASTER DRAWINGS FROM CALIFORNIA COLLECTIONS. The printing is by offset lithography with plates produced in 200 line screen. Printing is by California Printing Company, San Francisco. The type face is Times Roman, set by Spartan Typographers. Paper is Colophon Basis 80 Text and Basis 80 Cover.